THE CREDIT CARD GAME

How to Turn Your Credit Card into an Asset and not a Liability

DR. CHARLEY THOMAS

DEDICATION

To my son,

You are the reason I found the strength to change my life. Your love and presence motivated me to become the best version of myself. This book is a testament to the power of perseverance, and I hope it always inspires you to turn challenges into opportunities. You are my greatest asset.

With all my love,
Mom

CONTENTS

PREFACE

In today's world, achieving financial stability can seem out of reach, especially when credit card debt is always lurking in the background. For many people, including myself, credit cards often start as a necessary tool but quickly become a source of stress. Like so many others, I initially misunderstood the real potential of credit cards. This book, *The Credit Card Game: How to Turn Your Credit Card into an Asset and Not a Liability*, is a collection of my personal experiences, professional insights, and practical strategies that helped me shift credit cards from being a financial burden into a tool for growth.

I am Dr. Charley Thomas—a licensed pharmacist, an investor, and entrepreneur. My story isn't one of overnight success. It's one of persistence, learning, and facing life's challenges head-on. I grew up in poverty, where financial literacy was rarely discussed. To add to the difficulty, I became a single mother as a teenager, which made the path to financial independence even more complex.

At nineteen, I was paying 18% interest on an auto loan with no other credit to my name. I got the loan because I had a job and a steady work history, but I didn't fully understand what I was getting into. A year later, I got my first credit card with a $500 limit, and I felt empowered, even though I didn't have a plan for using it beyond buying gas. By paying off the card monthly and being responsible, my credit limit rose to $5,500 within three years.

Not long after, I was laid off unexpectedly. With no income apart from unemployment—around $100 a week—my savings ran out quickly, and I had to rely on that credit card just to survive. At that moment, I realized that financial security couldn't be based on luck or circumstances; it had to be built. I knew that education was my ticket to a better life, but navigating forward felt like climbing a mountain.

Before I became a mother, I had attended college, but toward the end of my pregnancy, I had to cut back on courses. My status changed from full-time to part-time, and I lost my eligibility for loans and scholarships. This forced me to make the hardest decision, and I dropped out, owing a hefty tuition balance. My dream, however, was to return to school and become a pharmacist so I could build a better future for my son and me. But without good credit, everything seemed more complicated. I faced high interest rates just like my initial auto loan, and I had very few options. It often felt like I was trapped in a cycle of financial hardship that would never end.

Despite these early setbacks, I didn't give up. I went back to school, earning both a business degree and a Doctor of Pharmacy degree. Also, I started teaching myself about finance, the stock market, and real estate. My motivation was simple: I wanted to change my life and ensure my son and future generations had better opportunities. As I progressed in my career as a pharmacist, I saw that financial struggles weren't confined to people with low incomes. Even among peers earning six figures—and even millionaires I encountered—there was a common problem: a lack of financial management skills, particularly when it came to credit cards.

Credit cards, often seen as a one-way ticket to debt, were at the center of much of this misunderstanding. I knew this firsthand.

I had once been trapped by credit card debt and high-interest rates, but over time I learned how to manage credit cards differently. I dove deep into budgeting, spending strategies, and credit management, first for myself and then for the people around me. What began as a personal journey became an effort to teach friends, family, and others how to navigate credit card debt and use credit to build a solid financial foundation.

Through consistent learning and action, I was able to shift the way I used credit cards, turning them into assets that allowed me to build savings, invest, and ultimately improve not only my life but the lives of those I helped. Today, I've been fortunate to assist others in securing over a million dollars in credit card funding, helping them find financial stability and success.

This book is more than just a guide—it's a reflection of what financial education can do. Whether you're feeling buried by credit card debt or looking to maximize the potential of your credit for future growth, *The Credit Card Game* offers practical, real-world strategies that can help you turn credit cards into valuable financial tools. I invite you to take this journey with me and learn how to rewrite your financial story, just as I did.

These early experiences with financial challenges taught me one thing: credit cards can be powerful tools or dangerous traps, depending on how you use them. In this book, I'll show you how to master the game and make credit cards work for you.

INTRODUCTION

Welcome to *The Credit Card Game*, where your spending habits and financial decisions can make or break your financial future. Credit cards have a bad reputation for being a liability. This is with good reason. According to consumer debt data from the Federal Reserve Bank of New York, in the second quarter of 2023, Americans' credit card debt hit $1.031 trillion. And indeed, they can be a source of stress, debt, and financial insecurity if not used responsibly and strategically. This is why debt collection, consolidation, and credit repair companies continue to make millions of dollars a year. Credit cards can be a liability if you do not know how credit cards work. *The Credit Card Game* is here to remove that bad reputation and teach you to strategically use your credit cards to maximize rewards, benefits, and financial advantages. Turning your credit card from a liability into an asset.

Most people consider managing credit cards a battle, but it's not a battle. It's a game. When you know how to play it, you will win. Just like any sports game requires discipline, strategy, and skill from its players, turning your credit card into an asset is a game that requires careful planning and execution. The key is understanding the game's rules and how to play it effectively.

The playbook for *The Credit Card Game* will provide you with a strategic plan containing offensive and defensive plays. And before we start to play the game, we must understand the rules and our opponent. That is the only way to win.

Credit card companies make money by charging interest on the balances that customers carry over from month to month. This is an important fact to know because the bank is your opponent. In this game, you do not want your opponent to score. According to the Federal Reserve, the average interest rate in November 2022 for U.S. credit card balances was 20.4%. If you do not pay your balance in full each month, the credit card company will multiply the balance each day by a ***daily interest rate*** and add that to what you owe. Let's calculate a balance with the average annual percentage rate (APR) of 20.4%. The daily rate is your APR divided by 365. For example, the daily rate for an APR of 20.4% is 0.056%. Just imagine having a balance of $10,000, and the daily rate on this amount is $560. This means the average person pays 20.4% in interest if their credit card balance is not paid in full. This is money you are throwing away, and you are playing to lose.

Coaches use playbooks to help win games. The players study and practice the plays in the playbook to improve their performance and increase their chances of clinching the victory. As with sports, *The Credit Card Game* has a playbook we must understand to win.

The Rules of the Credit Card Game

Like any game, credit cards have rules you must follow if you want to win. First, you should know how a credit card works, its terms and conditions, credit limit, interest rate, and payment due date. Understanding these rules can help you avoid penalties, fees, and other pitfalls that can hurt your credit score and financial health. In addition, having this knowledge enables you to create a strategy for using your credit card(s) to your advantage.

Once you understand the rules of the game, it's time to develop a strategy. For example, in sports, teams have specific plays and techniques they use to score points and win games. Similarly, you need to develop a strategy to turn your credit card into an asset. This means setting a spending plan, establishing payment goals, and choosing the right credit cards for your needs. Your plan should take into account your income, expenses, and financial goals, and it should help you use your credit cards to build your credit score and improve your financial health.

Discipline is the key to success in sports and the credit card game. In basketball, for instance, players must practice regularly and maintain good physical and mental health to perform at their best. Likewise, you must practice good financial habits and be disciplined in using your credit cards. This means paying your bills on time and in full, keeping your balance(s) low, and avoiding unnecessary purchases. By practicing discipline and self-control, you can avoid falling into debt and damaging your credit score (losing the game).

Just as athletes need to learn from their mistakes and make adjustments, you must be willing to adapt and make changes to your credit card strategy as required. To illustrate, if you find that your spending habits are getting out of hand, you may need to adjust your spending plan and reevaluate your financial goals.

Playing Offense

You must play offense in the credit card game. It's the key to turning your credit card into an asset. Playing offense is all about financial growth and benefits. It involves maximizing rewards, leveraging promotions, strategic spending, building credit, and investing. It takes proactive steps to make the most out of your credit card usage to improve your financial health. This means choosing the right credit card for your spending habits and using it strategically to earn rewards and building your credit to buy assets. For example, a credit card offering travel rewards may be the best option if you travel frequently. Alternatively, if you spend a lot on groceries and gas, a credit card that offers cash back on those purchases may be a better choice. Now, you are scoring points to win the game.

Playing Defense

In addition to playing offense, it is also important to play defense. Playing defense means taking proactive steps to safeguard your financial well-being by avoiding debt, making on-time payments, monitoring spending, and protecting your credit score. This is all about risk minimization and financial security.

Playing to Win

When you play the credit card game to win, you're using your credit card as a tool to improve your financial health. This includes financial planning, credit score optimization, maximizing rewards, sign-up bonuses, redeeming strategically, and using introductory offers to create cash flow. Playing to win in the credit card game requires discipline, financial responsibility, and a thorough understanding of its landscape. It's essential to stay organized, track your spending, pay your bills on time, and avoid carrying high-interest debt.

Playing to Lose

Playing to lose in the credit card game means using your credit card in ways that harm your overall financial health. It involves making decisions that can lead to credit card debt and high-interest charges. This includes making purchases you can't afford, missing payments, paying only the minimum, late payments, ignoring card terms, lack of financial planning, ignoring credit score impact, and maxing out your credit limit. Playing to lose can severely damage your credit score and overall financial health. Therefore, it's important to avoid playing to lose in the credit card game.

Building a Winning Strategy

Like in sports, building a winning strategy in the credit card game requires a combination of offense and defense. This means choosing the right credit card for your spending habits, using it strategically to earn rewards, and paying your balance in full each month to avoid interest charges. You also need to monitor your credit score and credit report to ensure there are no errors or fraudulent activity. It's a disciplined approach aimed at using credit cards as an effective financial tool to achieve long-term financial goals. A solid strategy will help you win the credit card game and turn your credit card into an asset.

Avoiding Pitfalls

Playing the credit card game can be challenging. Financial vigilance and responsible credit card management will help you avoid its many pitfalls. It's crucial to establish a well-structured spending plan and adhere to it diligently. Steer clear of common traps by using credit cards only for planned and essential expenses while resisting impulse purchases that could lead to overspending. Timely payments are non-negotiable, so setting up payment reminders or automatic payments will prevent late fees and protect your credit score. Avoid the costly burden of high-interest debt by consistently paying your credit card balances in full each month or explore balance transfers for existing high-interest debt. Maintain a low credit utilization ratio by keeping balances well below your credit limits to protect your credit score. Always read the fine print of credit card terms and conditions to make informed decisions and avoid unexpected fees or changes. Regularly monitoring your accounts for unauthorized charges and staying aware of how credit card usage affects your credit score can help you maintain a strong financial footing. Lastly, remember to use credit cards as financial tools, not crutches. Prioritize long-term financial stability over short-term convenience.

Credit cards don't have to be a liability. By treating credit card usage like a game, you can turn your credit card into an asset. This involves understanding the rules of the game, playing offense and defense, building a winning strategy, and avoiding pitfalls. If you follow the strategies in *The Credit Card Game*, you will improve your financial health and turn your credit card into an asset.

CHAPTER 1

KNOWING WHY YOU'RE APPLYING FOR A CREDIT CARD MATTERS

In the credit card game, your 'why' isn't just a question. It's the driving force that turns a financial liability into an asset.

—Dr. Charley Thomas

It feels like yesterday when I received my very first preapproved credit card offer in the mail from Capital One Bank. After opening that envelope, I was jumping for joy, as though I had won the MEGA Millions. My excitement was simply driven by the offer, as I had no real purpose for this credit card. I did not know why I needed it, nor did I have a clue about how credit cards work. Most importantly, I did not take the time to think about how it would impact me. During my teens and part of my young adult life, I was taught that credit wasn't necessary, and at the time it wasn't. I lived in a housing project and received benefits from the supplemental nutrition assistance program (SNAP). My essential needs were covered by government assistance. I didn't need credit or credit cards for anything in my life, or so I thought. Now you can see why I was so excited by just getting a pre-approved letter.

Like most people, I was blindly applying for a credit card and too focused on getting approved. To me, I felt like I had made it. No one around me was taking advantage of the benefits of credit and credit cards. I remember sitting down to apply for the offer, and it was approved within seconds. The message read: *Congratulations, you are approved for a credit limit of $500. You will receive your new card in the mail within 3-5 business days.* Any other time, I would only check my mailbox once a week. But this time around, I was anxiously checking the mailbox every day, starting from the moment they said I was approved.

I know $500 is not much money. However, it was plenty at that time in my life. My salary then was slightly higher than the income limits permitted to continue receiving government assistance for housing and food. This meant I no longer had a safety net. Why am I telling you this? Because more than 60% of Americans are living paycheck to paycheck, and I was included in that number. Most people get into credit card debt by overspending. Having no financial education and coming from a life with a safety net put me at a disadvantage and increased my chances of accumulating debt. Before applying for my first credit card, I did not ask myself pertinent questions about its use. I did not understand the credit card game. Therefore, I was on the path to turning my credit card into a liability.

We all are targeted for credit cards in some shape or form. From the mail pre-approvals, email ads, social media, and many other ways. Credit card companies often market their products aggressively, highlighting the benefits while downplaying the potential risks.

Without having a clear understanding of your objectives, you may fall into the trap of applying for a card solely based on promotional offers or status.

Why Knowing Why You're Getting a Credit Card Matters

Let's talk about credit cards, a payment card that allows the cardholder to borrow funds from a financial institution, the issuer. It gives a cardholder the convenience of accessing money for whatever they need whenever they need within the credit limit. The funds automatically renew as the borrower repays the debt. This is known as revolving credit, which allows the cardholder to access funds up to a predetermined amount, known as the credit limit.

However, the funds must be paid back. It's not free money. When a purchase is made using a credit card, the cardholder is essentially taking out a short-term loan from the credit card issuer. If the balance is paid in full by the due date, no interest will be charged on the amount borrowed. However, if the balance is not paid in full, interest charges will accrue on the outstanding balance.

Imagine credit cards as a two-sided tool. When you use them wisely and with a clear goal, they can help secure your financial future. But if you're not careful, they can lead to financial trouble. The secret to handling credit cards well is to have a strong reason for having one.

This brings me to the first lesson in the credit card game: Before you act, ask yourself, "Why am I getting this credit card?"

The Temptation of Credit Cards

Credit cards are like a tempting offer that seems too good to resist. They promise you the ability to get what you want right now, even if you can't afford it. Imagine you get an offer for a credit card with a high spending limit. The advertisements show you luxurious vacations, fancy dinners, and the latest gadgets, all the things you want. It's like seeing your favorite sport on TV and believing you can become a pro athlete without training.

With a credit card, you can buy things immediately, without waiting to save money. It's as if you can score a winning goal in a game without practicing. The problem is: using credit cards this way often leads to debt, and you are playing to lose. Credit cards have hidden costs, like interest charges and fees. These costs can turn your desire for instant rewards into a financial problem. It's like thinking you're winning a game, when in reality, you're falling behind.

To resist the temptation of credit cards, you must understand how they work and have a clear plan for your finances. Just like in sports, you need discipline, practice, and a long-term strategy to succeed.

The Two Sides of the Court

I am not here to penalize your desires or dreams. After all, even star athletes dream of achieving greatness. But I am here to guide you toward a game plan that ensures those dreams become reality without fouling out of your financial league.

When you apply for a credit card, you find yourself at a critical juncture, much like a pivotal moment in a sports match.

The Strategic Play (Asset): This is the path least traveled–the one that separates the champions from the rest. It starts with a clear game plan in mind. You're applying for a credit card because you recognize its value in your financial field. You've pinpointed specific goals or needs—building credit, earning rewards, managing emergencies, creating passive income, starting a business, or consolidating existing debt. Each swipe/tap of the card is a calculated move in your financial playbook, a step toward helping make your financial situation stronger.

The Impulsive Turnover (Liability): This path is crowded with noise and instant gratification. Here, credit cards become tools for quick satisfaction. The "why" often fades into the background, eclipsed by the "why not?" You apply for a card without a game plan, which becomes a tactic to give in to momentary desires. The result? Penalties in the form of debts that stack up, interest accrues, and your financial scoreboard takes a beating.

The Importance of Knowing Why

We live in a world of instant gratification. With so many social media outlets and influencers promoting financial advice, it's easy to make an impulsive fumble. Recently, I saw a video about getting a Navy Federal credit card with a credit limit of $25,000. While anyone would want to get their hands on a card with a $25,000 credit limit, this wasn't a Navy Federal promotional video. Instead, it was a credit repair company on social media. This promo ad motivated many followers to comment about wanting to sign up and get approved for the $25,000 credit limit. However, if this ad were valid, you would pay for the company's services to repair your credit and get approved for the credit card.

The questions not asked or discussed were:

1. What would be the real purpose of getting this credit card?
2. How will it impact you?
3. Is there any benefit to this card besides having access to a large amount of money?
4. Do you have experience responsibly managing a large amount of money?
5. Would you have the funds to pay the interest on the card even if you used only 10% of the $25,000?

It is important to ask yourself these questions, as it will be a costly mistake if you don't. Nearly 40% of American credit card owners carry a balance on their credit card month to month. Furthermore, 43% don't know their interest rate (APR). During consultation, nearly 95% of my clients did not know their interest rates or that credit card interest compounds daily. Knowing why you want a credit card is like having a game plan that can make a big difference in how you handle it.

The Importance of Purpose

Before you even start the credit card application process, take a moment to reflect on your financial goals and needs. Ask yourself why you want a credit card. Understanding your purpose can help you choose the right card and set responsible usage boundaries. The reasons differ, depending on where you are mentally and/or financially.

Some of us apply without fully understanding why and how it will affect our finances in the long term. Therefore, it's essential to take the time to evaluate our motivations and make informed decisions when applying for a credit card. Rather than just getting excited and randomly applying for a credit card with our fingers crossed, we must ask ourselves a few questions:

1. Why am I getting this credit card?
2. What's my credit card's purpose?
3. How will it impact me when I am approved?

Why am I Getting this Credit Card?

I acquire credit cards to establish and strengthen my credit history. Also, I understand that a well-managed credit history is an essential component of my financial game plan. This will enable me to qualify for better mortgage rates and improve my financial standing.

What's My Credit Card's Purpose?

The primary purpose of my credit cards is to demonstrate my ability to manage credit. I use my credit cards for everyday expenses, making sure I pay the balance in full each month. My intention is to showcase my responsible credit usage, not accumulate debt.

How Will It Impact Me When I am Approved?

Being approved for credit cards allows me to start building a credit history. My credit score improves as I consistently make on-time payments and maintain low credit card balances. A higher credit score positions me favorably when seeking mortgage financing for my income properties. It can save me thousands of dollars in interest costs over the life of the mortgages.

Results and Future Plans

Over time, I successfully built a strong credit profile. My diligent efforts resulted in an excellent credit score, and I qualified for mortgages with favorable interest rates.

With my credit cards as a stepping stone, I confidently entered the real estate market. I acquired my first income property and began generating passive income. As my portfolio grows, my creditworthiness remains a powerful tool, allowing me to easily secure financing for additional properties.

Credit Cards as Building Blocks for Real Estate Success

As a teen mom who once lived a life of poverty, I was determined to break generational curses with a vision of financial independence. I understood that achieving my goal of acquiring income properties required a strategic approach. To navigate the journey successfully, I decided to leverage credit cards as building blocks for my credit profile and finance my real estate endeavors in the future.

I had three goals:

1. **Build a Strong Credit Profile:** My starting point is understanding the importance of credit in the world

of real estate. A strong credit profile will enable me to secure favorable financing terms for my investment properties.

2. **Acquire Income Properties:** My ultimate goal is to own multiple income-generating properties. These properties will not only provide financial security but also serve as a source of passive income for my son's future.

3. **Minimize Interest Costs:** I recognize the significance of minimizing interest costs when investing in real estate. Lower interest rates mean higher cash flow from my properties.

Credit cards can be valuable tools in building credit history and financial credibility which are essential for obtaining mortgages and financing real estate deals. My game plan revolved around using credit cards strategically to achieve my goals.

Understanding why you are getting credit cards and having a clear game plan make all the difference. It was a critical step in my journey toward achieving financial independence through real estate investments.

As we've seen through the case study and the exploration of the importance of purpose, your motivation for obtaining a credit card matters profoundly. Remember, the temptation of credit cards can be intense. Still, with a well-defined purpose, responsible usage, and a strategic mindset, you can transform your credit card into a valuable asset, ultimately turning it into a winning player on your financial team.

In the upcoming chapters, we'll explore the strategies, tips, and knowledge that will help you win the credit card game and turn your credit card into an asset rather than a liability.

Chapter 1 Questions

1. What is a credit card?

2. Explain revolving credit.

3. What is a strategic play and an impulsive fumble in the credit card game? Why is this important to know?

4. What three questions should you ask yourself before applying for a credit card?

5. In the case study, how did knowing 'why' help her set goals and create a game plan?

CHAPTER 2

UNDERSTANDING CREDIT CARDS

Credit cards are financial tools that can be used to either benefit or harm an individual's financial situation. The decision on how to use a credit card ultimately lies with the individual, and their choices can turn it into either an asset or a liability.

—Dr. Charley Thomas

I remember sitting and covering my face with my hands, crying about my future. After days of wondering what I would do with my life, I felt stuck and hopeless. A single mother whose child's father was in federal prison. I had no real career in place, and I had recently been laid off. Moreover, I was a college dropout. This wasn't always the case. Just a few years before, I was enrolled at Xavier University of Louisiana (XULA) on a scholarship, pursuing my dream of becoming a pharmacist. The trajectory of my life changed swiftly.

It wasn't easy trying to grasp what was happening to me. It was almost as if I was having an out-of-body experience. But at that time, I could not focus on myself. My goals were to create a loving environment for my son and provide for him.

There were so many emotions at that moment, but I needed a plan to move forward—a solid plan. Setting my emotions aside, I arrived at the only logical answer: go back to school to complete my pharmacy degree. The major obstacle was that I owed XULA a hefty bill for previous tuition. I could not return without paying my past-due balance. When I dropped out of college, I forfeited my scholarship. How was I going to pay this tuition? I burst into tears and thought, *I have no money, and I don't like the direction of my future.* Boy, oh boy, was I crying a lot. I needed this to happen. Suddenly, I stopped crying and shifted my thinking. That's when I got the idea to use my credit card to pay for it. I did not have a repayment plan, but I knew I was going to do it.

After completing the payment and finally becoming a student again at XULA, I spoke with my pre-pharmacy counselor to review my transcript. The moment I walked across the seal of her door, she recognized me. I was stunned. She told me she didn't think I was coming back.

I said, "But I told you I was coming back."

My return sparked her interest in me, and I am grateful. She treated my son like her grandson, even keeping him in her office during finals week while I took my exams.

Once I was allowed to return to XULA, I started my undergraduate (pre-pharmacy) classes in the summer. I was so happy to be back on campus to begin the journey to my new life. However, I was denied on my first attempt at applying to pharmacy school. At that moment, my GPA and profile were not competitive. Nevertheless, I did not let that kill my spirit. I still believed in my dream. So, I decided to get my chemistry degree and then reapply.

The following year, I applied to pharmacy school. This time, I was on track to graduate with my bachelor's in chemistry. My GPA looked good, and I was a potential pharmacy school candidate. I received an acceptance letter this time and was jumping for joy. However, I was accepted on a contingency basis. I had to enroll in an accelerated matriculation program the summer before my fall semester as a pharmacy student. The program was very intense. There was no turning back now, and I could see my life changing in front of me.

My credit card has allowed me to see my life differently now. I had wisely utilized my financial tool as an asset to invest in myself.

Credit cards are financial tools that can be used to either benefit or harm an individual's financial situation. The decision on how to use a credit card ultimately lies with the individual, and their choices can turn it into either an asset or a liability.

Understanding Credit Cards

We're diving into the world of credit cards, where the goal is playing to win. Understanding credit cards is an essential financial skill that can help you make informed financial decisions. Think of it as learning the rules of a game, except this game is all about managing your money wisely. Did you know that a whopping **82% of Americans** have at least one credit card? But here's the thing: **3 out of 5 people** end up in credit card debt. Yikes! Globally, people are swiping their cards to the tune of **$40 trillion**, with the U.S. racking up a hefty **$9.5 trillion**. And get this: **1 in 3 Americans** owe more on their credit cards than they have saved up. Crazy, right? Before you can turn your credit card into a helpful tool, it's crucial to understand the basics. So, let's learn how to play the credit card game like pros and break down the playbook together before we hit the court!

Decoding the terms:

- Interest rate or annual percentage rate (APR)
- Credit limits
- Credit card balance
- Fees

Interest rate or Annual Percentage Rate (APR)

The interest rate is the cost of borrowing money on your credit card. It is expressed as an **annual percentage rate (APR)**, which can vary depending on your credit card type and creditworthiness. Understanding your credit card's APR is essential, as it affects the interest you'll pay if you carry a balance. The APR is calculated based on the amount you owe on your card at the end of each billing cycle. For example, if you borrow $1,000 at an interest rate of 10%, you'll have to pay back $1,100 ($1,000 + $100 in interest). Interest rates can vary depending on factors such as the type of loan, creditworthiness, and market conditions.

Credit card companies offer two types of interest rates:

1. **Fixed:** A fixed interest rate remains the same for the life of your credit card.
2. **Variable:** A variable interest rate can change depending on market conditions.

It's important to note that credit card interest rates are typically higher than other types of loans (mortgages or car loans) because credit card loans are unsecured (not backed by collateral like a house or car).

Credit Limits

Your **credit limit** is the maximum amount of money you can borrow on your credit card. It is determined by the credit card issuer based on your credit score, income, and other factors. It's important to stay within your credit limit because you may be charged an over-the-limit fee if you go over. Additionally, going over your credit limit can negatively impact your credit score.

Credit Card Balance

Your credit card balance is the amount of money you owe the credit card issuer. It includes any unpaid purchases, cash advances, balance transfers, and fees charged to your credit card account. It can fluctuate over time as you use it for purchases and other transactions. To understand your credit card balance, you must also understand your **billing cycle**, **due date**, and **grace period**.

The credit card billing cycle is important because it determines the period during which you are required to pay your credit card bill and affects the interest charges and fees that may be applied to your account.

The billing cycle is the length of time between your credit card statement dates. This is typically around 30 days but can vary depending on the card issuer. During this time, you can make purchases using your credit card, and the issuer will keep a running balance of your transactions.

At the end of the billing cycle, the issuer will send you a statement that lists all transactions you made during that time, along with the minimum payment due and the due date. The minimum payment is the minimum you can pay on time to keep your account in good standing. In the credit card game we do not want to pay the minimum payment; we want the balance paid in full each month. The due date varies depending on the issuer and the terms of your card agreement, but it is typically around 21-25 days after the statement closing date. If you do not pay your balance in full by the due date, interest charges will be applied to your account.

Understanding your billing cycle can help you avoid interest charges and fees by paying your balance in full and on time. You can also use your billing cycle to your advantage by timing your purchases and payments to maximize rewards and minimize interest charges.

The chart is an example of a bill which shows the
Billing cycle, due date and grace period.

Fees

Credit card companies charge various fees that can add up quickly if you're not careful. Some of the most common fees you should look out for are:

Late fees: If you don't pay at least the minimum amount due on your credit card by the due date, you'll be charged a late payment fee.

Annual fees: Some credit cards charge a yearly fee for the privilege of using the card. Make sure the card's benefits outweigh the annual fee.

Balance transfer fees: If you transfer a balance from one credit card to another, you may be charged a fee for the transfer.

Cash advance fees: If you use your credit card to get cash, you'll be charged a cash advance fee. This is typically a percentage of the amount you withdraw.

Foreign transfer fees: If you use your credit card to make purchases in a foreign currency, you may be charged a foreign transaction fee.

2023 Totals Year-to-Date	
Total fees charged in 2023	$0.00
Total interest charged in 2023	$0.00

Year-to-date totals do not reflect any fee or interest refunds
you may have received.

INTEREST CHARGES

Your **Annual Percentage Rate (APR)** is the annual interest rate on your account.

Balance Type	Annual Percentage Rate (APR)	Expiration Date	Balance Subject to Interest Rate	Interest Charges
PURCHASES				
Purchases	0.00% (d)	11/23/24	- 0 -	- 0 -
Purchases	20.49% (d)	-	- 0 -	- 0 -
CASH ADVANCES				
Cash Advances	29.99%(v)(d)	11/23/24	- 0 -	- 0 -
Cash Advances	29.99%(v)(d)	-	- 0 -	- 0 -
BALANCE TRANSFERS				
Balance Transfers	0.00% (d)	11/23/24	- 0 -	- 0 -
Balance Transfers	20.49% (d)	-	- 0 -	- 0 -

30 Days in Billing Period

(v) = Variable Rate
(d) = Daily Balance Method (including new transactions)
(a) = Average Daily Balance Method (including new transactions)
Please see Information About Your Account section for the Calculation of Balance Subject to Interest Rate, Annual Renewal Notice, How to Avoid Interest on Purchases, and other important information, as applicable.

*If you change your payment due date, the date your promotional rate(s) ends also changes. Please be assured, the promotional rate will last for the time period promised in your offer.

The chart is the last part of the credit card statement that shows the fees associated with that credit card.

It's important to read the fine print on your credit card agreement to know what fees to expect. Some credit cards may waive certain fees, like foreign transaction fees and late payment fees (based on certain circumstances). It is always worth shopping around to find the best deal. Understanding these terms can help you make informed financial decisions and improve your overall financial health.

Chapter 2 Questions

1. True or false. Credit cards are financial tools that can be used to either benefit or harm an individual's financial situation.

2. Why is it important to know your credit limit, and how does exceeding it affect your credit score?

3. Define the term APR.

4. Why is it important to know your credit card billing cycle?

5. What happens when you do not pay your statement balance by your due date?

CHAPTER 3

RULES OF THE CREDIT CARD GAME

Credit cards are a financial game. To make them an asset, you must learn the rules of the game.

—Dr. Charley Thomas

Credit cards are a financial game. Just like any other game in life, it's important that you understand the system to be successful at it. Not understanding the rules and putting them in place is why most Americans are in debt. To make credit cards an asset, you must learn the rules of the game and apply them. Knowing the rules but not applying them is another reason most Americans are in debt.

The following seven rules will help you achieve success with using credit cards:

Rule 1. Know your credit score: The foundation of the game

Your credit score is the MVP (most valuable player) of the credit card game. It's like knowing your team's ranking before a match. So, what exactly is a credit score? A credit score is a numerical representation of your creditworthiness. Our credit scores have a significant influence on our lives. It can determine where you live, the cost of car insurance, interest on money borrowed, your ability to get credit cards and other loans, as well as the terms and interest rates. Having a low credit score can be expensive. A higher score means better opportunities, like getting approved for premium cards with top-notch perks.

Factors such as payment history, credit utilization, length of credit history, types of credit, and new credit impact your credit score. Lenders use credit scores to assess your creditworthiness and ability to repay debt. Your credit score is typically grouped into categories or ranges.

The following credit score chart details the general categories and ranges:

Credit Score Chart	
Categories	Range
Excellent	800 and above
Very Good	740 to 799
Good	670 to 739
Fair	580 to 669
Poor	579 and below

Excellent credit

A credit score of 800 or above is considered excellent. People with excellent credit are typically regarded as low-risk borrowers and may have access to the best interest rates and credit terms.

Very Good credit

A credit score between 740 and 799 is considered very good. People with very good credit are generally seen as moderate-risk borrowers and may have access to favorable interest rates and credit terms.

Good credit

A credit score between 670 and 739 is considered good credit. People with good credit are considered higher-risk borrowers and may have more difficulty obtaining credit or pay higher interest rates.

Fair credit

A credit score between 580 and 669 is considered fair credit. People with fair credit scores may have difficulty obtaining credit or may have to pay higher interest rates and fees than those with higher credit scores.

Poor credit

A credit score below 580 is considered poor credit. People with poor credit scores may have difficulty obtaining credit, be required to pay very high interest rates and fees, or not get approved for credit.

Knowing your credit score is crucial in the credit card game because it is the foundation for your financial decisions and actions. Your credit score reflects your creditworthiness and how responsibly you manage your debts and finances.

Here's why it's important:

Access to Credit

A good credit score opens doors to better credit card offers and lower interest rates. You're more likely to qualify for premium credit cards with lucrative rewards and perks with a higher score.

Financial Opportunities

A high credit score grants you access to credit cards and other financial opportunities, such as mortgages, auto loans, and personal loans that can be used strategically to build wealth and assets.

Interest Rates and Fees

Your credit score influences the interest rates and fees associated with your credit cards. A higher score means you're more likely to receive lower interest rates and fewer fees, saving you money in the long run.

Credit Card Approval

When applying for a new credit card, lenders assess your credit score to determine your creditworthiness. A good score increases your chances of approval, allowing you to access new credit lines and potentially improve your credit utilization ratio.

Credit Utilization

Your credit score is impacted by your credit utilization ratio, which is the amount of credit you're using compared to your total available credit. Understanding your score can help you manage your credit utilization effectively, which is a key factor in maintaining a healthy credit profile.

In essence, knowing your credit score enables you to make informed decisions, optimize your credit card usage, and ultimately turn your credit card into an asset rather than a liability in the credit card game. It's the first rule because it sets the groundwork for wise financial management and paves the way toward achieving your financial goals.

Rule 2. Budgeting and paying in full (money management): Strategic gameplay (responsible credit card use)

Budgeting and fully paying your debt form the cornerstone of responsible credit card use and strategic money management. Picture this as your offensive strategy. Budgeting is like designing your playbook by setting the plays for your financial game. Paying in full, that's executing those plays. Together, they form an unbeatable strategy that keeps your financial scoreboard in the black.

The following is a list of its benefits:

Avoiding Interest Charges

Budgeting and paying your credit card balance in full each month rewards you with interest-free charges on your purchases. This saves you money in the long run and prevents your credit card from becoming a liability due to accumulating debt.

Maintaining Financial Discipline

Budgeting helps you track your spending and ensure you only use your credit card for purchases you can afford. Paying your balance in full demonstrates financial discipline and responsibility, which are crucial for maintaining a healthy credit profile.

Avoiding Debt Accumulation

Paying your balance in full prevents debt from accumulating on your credit card. This helps you avoid the trap of revolving debt, where high-interest charges can quickly spiral out of control and turn your credit card into a liability.

Building Creditworthiness

Consistently paying your credit card balance in full demonstrates to lenders that you are a responsible borrower. This helps improve your credit score over time, making it easier to qualify for better credit card offers and other financial opportunities in the future.

Strategic Gameplay

Treating your credit card as a tool for strategic gameplay involves using it wisely to maximize rewards, cash back, or other benefits while minimizing costs. Budgeting and paying in full allow you to leverage your credit card strategically without falling into debt traps. Rule 2 helps effectively manage your finances while building creditworthiness.

Rule 3. Choose your credit card wisely

Picking the right credit card is like recruiting players for your team—you want a card that complements your strategy. Consider your spending habits and goals when choosing a card. Get the credit card that best fits your lifestyle.

The Importance of Choice

Imagine standing in front of a buffet spread, each dish more tantalizing than the last. You can select the dishes that appeal to your taste buds and dietary preferences. Similarly, choosing your credit card allows you to tailor your financial tools to your unique needs, preferences, and spending habits.

Maximizing Rewards and Benefits

One of the most significant advantages of choosing your credit card wisely is maximizing rewards and benefits. Just as selecting the perfect dish at the buffet can elevate your dining experience, choosing a credit card that aligns with your spending habits can unlock valuable rewards and perks. Whether it's earning cash back on everyday purchases, accruing travel points for your next adventure, or enjoying exclusive benefits like airport lounge access, the right credit card can enhance your financial journey and provide tangible value.

Minimizing Costs

While rewards and benefits are undoubtedly appealing, it's essential to consider the costs associated with your credit card choice. Much like scanning the menu for hidden fees or overpriced items, scrutinizing credit card terms and conditions can help you avoid unnecessary costs and fees. By selecting a card with favorable terms, lower fees, and competitive interest rates, you can minimize the financial burden of using credit and ensure that your card remains a valuable asset rather than a liability.

Tailoring Features to Your Needs

Beyond rewards and costs, choosing your credit card wisely involves considering the features and perks that matter most to you. Just as selecting a dish tailored to your dietary preferences can enhance your dining experience, choosing a credit card with features aligned with your lifestyle and priorities can amplify its value. Whether it's travel insurance for jet-setters, purchase protection for savvy shoppers, or zero foreign transaction fees for globetrotters, the right credit card features can cater to your unique needs and enhance your overall financial well-being.

Avoiding Temptations

Finally, choosing your credit card wisely involves exercising discipline and avoiding temptations that could lead to financial pitfalls. Like resisting the urge to indulge in every dish at the buffet, selecting a credit card that aligns with your financial goals and spending habits can help you stay on track and avoid overspending or accumulating debt. By resisting the allure of flashy sign-up bonuses or promotional offers that come with strings attached, you can ensure that your credit card remains a valuable asset that supports your financial objectives.

Rule 4. Maximize rewards

Maximizing rewards allows your money to work for you. I know it may sound crazy, but hear me out. Real estate, stocks, and business ownership are typical ways of letting your money become income-earning financial vehicles . Unfortunately, for many people (like myself), we are not taught to leverage our credit cards like stocks, real estate, and business ownership. So, how is this possible?

Every month we pay bills, which equates to money going out. Each swipe of your credit card must become a strategic move, an opportunity to accumulate rewards and bonuses that can potentially put you in the best position to use your credit card as an asset. Imagine this: With every grocery run, utility payment, or dining experience, you're not just spending money—you're earning rewards. Those rewards can be turned into an investment fund, savings fund, or even fund your next trip or much more.

The key to maximizing rewards lies in understanding your spending habits, selecting the right credit cards to match those habits, and staying disciplined in your usage to maximize earning potential. It's about making your money work harder for you and turning your regular expenses into a source of financial gain.

By leveraging your monthly expenses to earn valuable rewards and bonuses, you're not just spending money but investing in your financial future and unlocking a world of possibilities.

Rule 5. Avoid traps and pitfalls

Every game has its pitfalls, and the credit card game is no exception. Late payments, annual fees, hidden fees, not knowing your billing cycle. To avoid falling into these traps, you need to be smart and cautious. Start by reviewing the decoding terms from chapter two. Before jumping into any offer, take a moment to read the fine print and understand what you're getting into. Ask yourself questions like: *Is there an annual fee? What is the value of the points? How are the rewards accumulated?*

Another trap to watch out for is overspending. It's easy to get carried away with your credit card, especially when rewards or discounts are involved. But spending more than you can afford can lead to financial trouble. So, it's important to stick to a budget and only spend what you know you can pay off in full each month.

Lastly, be on the lookout for scams. In today's digital world, plenty of crooks are trying to trick you into giving them your personal information or money. So, always be cautious of suspicious emails, offers, or requests for your credit card details.

Staying aware by avoiding these common traps can keep your credit cards working for you instead of against you. Remember, in the credit card game, it's better to be safe than sorry. By following Rule 5, you can navigate the world of credit cards with confidence and peace of mind.

Rule 6. Monitoring and adapting

Success in the credit card game requires vigilance and adapting to changing circumstances. Regularly reviewing your statements, tracking your spending, and adjusting your strategy as needed are crucial for staying ahead of the game. For example, Mark notices a sudden change in his credit card balance due to unexpected expenses.

He adjusts his budget and spending habits accordingly to avoid overspending and maintains financial stability.

Rule 7. Turning the tide:
From liability to asset

The journey through Rules 1 to 6 sets the stage for the pivotal Rule 7: Turning the Tide. Each preceding rule, from knowing your credit score to monitoring and adapting, equips you with the skills and knowledge to transition your credit cards from liabilities to assets. Rule 7 represents a transformative moment where strategic financial management comes to fruition, enabling you to consolidate debt, optimize rewards, and build a positive credit history. By diligently following these rules, you not only navigate the complexities of the credit card game but also unlock the potential to achieve long-term financial stability and success.

Chapter 3 Questions

1. What role does knowing your credit score play in the credit card game? How does it impact your financial decisions?

2. How does budgeting and paying your credit card balance in full each month contribute to responsible credit card use and strategic money management?

3. What factors should you consider when choosing a credit card? Why is it important to select one that aligns with your lifestyle and spending habits?

4. How can you leverage your monthly expenses to maximize rewards and benefits with your credit card? Why is this strategy important for financial gain?

5. What common traps and pitfalls should you be aware of when using credit cards? How can you avoid falling into them to maintain financial stability and prevent debt accumulation?

6. What are the rules of the credit card game?

CHAPTER 4

BUILDING CREDIT: PLAYING TO WIN

A good credit score can help you qualify for better interest rates and terms, saving you money over the long run. The reality is most people use credit cards to build credit. Building credit with credit cards takes time and responsible use. Like anything great, this doesn't happen overnight.

—Dr. Charley Thomas

Car loans were the beginning of my building credit. The interest rate on my first car note was in double digits, about 18%. That was ridiculous. At the beginning of pharmacy school, I was driving an ancient car that cost no more than $3,000. It was functional enough to get me to and from school, though. I was introduced to this finance guy that my cousin knew to get this car. We thought he was very knowledgeable at the time, but I soon realized it was only because we weren't financially literate. We took this guy's word like the *Bible*.

From this experience, I learned that you should always have some idea of what you need from someone. Take some time to research which questions to ask.

I relied on this person to help me get car loans. It was helpful at the moment, and now I had a car. It was a Sunfire. We called her Sunny. She did not have a fully functional AC. If you have ever lived in New Orleans, you know it's humid. When it's hot, it's uncomfortably hot. I can remember my commute to school. I would keep a change of clothes in a duffel bag in the trunk of my car. Each day I was drenched in sweat and would have to take a mini bath before class.

Just thinking about those moments brings tears to my eyes. I did not let anything get in my way or make excuses. I just did what was needed to achieve my goals. The struggle was indeed a struggle.

The finance guy wasn't all bad because he introduced me to credit unions and the benefits of getting a low-interest personal loan to pay off debt from high interest. Gaining this knowledge helped me pay off debt quicker and more efficiently. I applied for a personal loan. The rate was 4%. This loan helped eliminate the compound interest from credit card debt and helped build my credit.

This is how I paid off my credit card debt. Now I'm in good standing. To get negative remarks removed from my credit history, I called Capital One. I was able to negotiate and help clear my record. This made me very happy and was the beginning of great credit, which opened doors. My credit score increased within the next 60-90 days.

I'm walking you through these phases because these are the steps you can also take to get out of credit card debt. A simple personal loan was the key to unlocking my credit potential. No matter what financial situation you are in, there is a solution.

Sunny eventually died, and now I needed a car. Now that my credit score was in the 700s, I was able to get a low-interest car loan. Nothing too expensive because my income was not enough. As my last year in pharmacy school approached, I lost track of my goals as I began comparing my life to how my peers were living. I felt like I did not want to just survive; I wanted to live well.

The first thing I did was upgrade my car. That was the dumbest idea ever. My partner at the time had such an extravagant lifestyle that it made my life feel small. I thought, *Damn, this man is really living.* He had exposed me to the finer things in life that I had never been exposed to, and I started to feel unhappy about my life. Initially, my new car purchase convinced me that I was really doing something, but now it looked as if I wasn't doing anything.

My mindset changed, and I compared my life to others instead of keeping my eye on the original goal. We can't judge our life based on someone else's life. But I was young, trying to figure my life out. I had never seen or experienced these opportunities and felt I was missing out, which caused me to lose focus. So although I had a fully functional car within my budget, I still went out and upgraded my car right before graduation day. It was my attempt at creating a lifestyle based on my projected salary, not my current earnings.

So instead of keeping my balance sheet in order, I began counting money I hadn't yet earned. We often add expenses based on projected earnings and forget we still need to save and invest. I adjusted my earnings without considering that I needed to pass my board exams first to practice as a pharmacist. Not only that, I wanted to look so fly—like I was, you know—doing it.

For graduation, I went shopping at Saks Fifth Avenue and fell in love with these Louboutins. The clerk gave me the advertised speech for their Saks Capital One credit card that would give me a discount on purchases. It's another Capital One card, but it's through Saks (co-branded credit card). I thought it was a great idea at the time because I would get a percentage off my purchase. Although I had started to improve my financial health, I still didn't quite understand credit cards and their purpose.

I applied and was approved, but the only benefit was a simple discount with no room for anything else. I still viewed credit cards as free money, not as an asset. This was not a great idea financially, and soon I realized that. I paid off the balance and closed the account within 45 days of opening it.

When we make financial decisions without a purpose, it can hurt us. Closing an account can hurt your credit score. Although my account was in good standing, my credit score still decreased. After a few months, my score increased, because I was paying down my loans.

Building Wealth

During my financial journey, I learned that real estate can effectively build wealth over the long term, as it provides several opportunities for capital appreciation and passive income generation. From that moment on, my primary financial goal was to obtain as many doors as possible to reach financial freedom and live my life peacefully and unapologetically.

Here's how my credit cards helped me purchase my first property. I eliminated using my debit card for anything, and my credit card became my bank account. I created my personal financial statement and paid all expenses with a credit card, making sure to monitor my cash flow. I was building a great credit profile, which is basically a requirement for obtaining loans, mortgages, and other forms of credit in the future.

A good credit score can help you qualify for better interest rates and terms, saving you money over the long run. The reality is most people use credit cards to build credit. However, building credit with credit cards takes time and responsible use.

Credit Score

In Chapter Three, we talked about the importance of credit scores. Credit scores are numerical ratings that summarize a person's creditworthiness. Lenders use credit scores to determine the likelihood that a borrower will repay their debts on time. There are different methods of calculating credit scores, but most use a combination of the following factors:

Payment History

This accounts for about **35%** of your credit score. Lenders want to see that you have a history of paying your bills on time, so they look at your payment history on loans, credit cards, and other forms of credit.

Amounts Owed

This accounts for about **30%** of your credit score. Lenders look at the amount of debt you have compared to your available credit. They want to see that you are not using too much of your available credit, which can suggest you are a higher credit risk.

Length of Credit History

This accounts for about **15%** of your credit score. Lenders like to see a long credit history because it indicates you have experience managing credit over time.

Credit Mix

This accounts for about **10%** of your credit score. Lenders look at your credit types, such as credit cards, car loans, and mortgages. A diverse mix of credit can indicate responsible credit management.

New Credit

This accounts for about **10%** of your credit score. Lenders look at how often you apply for new credit. Applying for too much credit in a short period can indicate financial stress and make you appear riskier to lenders.

Credit scores are typically calculated using a mathematical formula that assigns weights to these factors. The most commonly used credit scoring model is the FICO score, which ranges from 300 to 850. A higher credit score indicates a better credit risk, while a lower score indicates a higher credit risk.

How Credit Cards Help with Building Credit

Credit cards can play an important role in building credit because they are a form of revolving credit that can be used to demonstrate a consistent history of timely payments.

Here are some key ways that credit cards can help build credit:

Establishing Credit History

Credit cards can help establish a credit history for individuals who do not have any credit yet. By using a credit card responsibly and paying the bills on time each month, individuals can demonstrate to lenders that they are reliable borrowers.

Payment History

A good payment history is one of the most important factors in building credit. By making regular, on-time payments, individuals can show they are responsible with credit and can be trusted to repay debts in full.

Credit Utilization

Another critical factor in building credit is credit utilization, which refers to the amount of credit being used relative to the total credit limit. Keeping credit utilization under **30%** of the credit limit is generally recommended. I personally use a **10%** rule for credit utilization. By using a credit card responsibly and keeping the balance low, individuals can demonstrate that they are able to manage credit responsibly.

Length of Credit History

Credit cards can also help build credit by establishing a long credit history. The longer an individual has had credit, the better it looks to lenders. By using a credit card responsibly over time, individuals can build a more substantial credit history and demonstrate their creditworthiness.

It is important to note that using credit cards irresponsibly can have a negative impact on credit scores—playing to lose. Late payments, high balances, and frequent credit card applications can all harm credit scores. But if you are careful, using credit cards responsibly and paying bills on time each month is the easiest way to build credit effectively.

Chapter 4 Questions

1. Why do lenders use a credit score to determine a borrower's eligibility?

2. What percentage of your credit score amounts to your payment history?

3. How do you define credit card mix?

4. What is one of the most important factors in building credit?

5. Define credit utilization.

CHAPTER 5

SETTING FINANCIAL GOALS: BUILDING A WINNING STRATEGY

Financial success is not a matter of chance but of strategy. Like a skilled athlete prepares for victory, effective financial management requires setting clear goals and executing a winning game plan.

—Dr. Charley Thomas

Bang!Bang!Bang! A loud noise rumbled from the front door. I was getting my son dressed and packed for daycare. "Open up. It's the police!" the officer replied.

Shortly after, the police kicked in the door and rushed inside with barking dogs and guns drawn. They were looking for my son's father. He hadn't reported to his probation officer and was suspected of selling illegal narcotics. Our home was turned upside down, and my son's father was carried away in handcuffs for a probation violation, which landed him in jail for a while. What a way to start the day. But at that moment, I knew I needed to make a decision for my son's well-being.

I did not report to work that day. Instead, I spent it looking for somewhere safe to call home, just for the two of us, mommy and son. Finally, I found a lovely mixed-income apartment complex that offered income-based units to a limited number of renters. I applied, and within two days I received a call welcoming me to my new home. The apartment was an end unit on the top floor with a fantastic view. Security was top-notch, with keypad entry and a parking garage underneath. My son always refers to it as the hotel.

After that call, I immediately rented a U-Haul truck and just threw all my belongings into the back without packing anything. I wanted a new start, and I needed it badly. I did not want anyone to know where I was staying. I called my uncle to help with the heavy lifting. A close friend called and heard the distress in my voice and popped up to help as well.

We were now safe, and I had removed us from that environment. I felt a sense of relief; I had found my safe haven. Unfortunately, that safe haven soon came to an end when I had to make the decision to downgrade after getting laid off.

My only source of income was eliminated. I had searched for employment with no success, so now I was receiving unemployment, which wasn't enough to pay bills. In Chapter Two, I mentioned how I used my credit card to pay my owed tuition to Xavier University of Louisiana to pursue my pharmacist dream. Here's where the story comes full circle.

Making the decision to focus on getting my doctorate degree was the best thing I could do to provide my son with opportunities instead of growing up poor with limited resources. I believe you are a product of your environment, meaning your upbringing influences your decisions. Also, I believe that knowledge and education can shape you. Let's look at my previous decisions: teen mom dating a drug dealer. That was the reality of my life at the time, and it needed to change.

The first step was leaving that environment and moving us somewhere safe, away from his father. I checked that off the list, but now that my financial situation had changed, I was unsure of what to do next.

Can you imagine having to decide to move away from a place that was your safe haven? It was a hard decision to make, but necessary to align with my goals and finances. I was now creating a budget. But first, I had to eliminate my biggest monthly expense—my rent.

My grandmother owned a double shotgun-style property in the ninth ward of New Orleans. If you are not familiar with a shotgun home, let me tell you about it. There are no doors to separate the rooms; just a straight walk through the entire house, with the bathroom in the middle and the kitchen at the very back of the home. Each side had two bedrooms with one bathroom.

My grandmother lived on one side, and the other side was left vacant and uninhabitable. Hurricane Katrina had damaged the house. Financial literacy was not a strong suit for us; however, we knew enough to survive. The home was paid for by the disaster relief fund. For years, one side was vacant and partially finished.

To downgrade and eliminate some monthly expenses, I asked my grandmother if I could live on the vacant side. I offered to complete the remaining renovations to make that side comfortable to live in. I planned to use my tax refund for the repairs to help decrease my monthly expenses to fit my budget. She was hesitant at first but ultimately said yes. So I went down to city hall and paid for the permits, electrical, and completion of the AC unit setup.

Upon doing that, my grandmother said, "Charley, I need you to pay a deposit." Here I am thinking my grandmother was going to help me out. But actually she saw my moving in as a money-making opportunity. This placed our relationship in an uneasy space. I said, "Grandmother, I have to finish the rest of this side to make it livable, and you are asking me for a deposit?" I could not understand it, but it was her property. Then I discovered that the property taxes were so far behind, and the house had almost been sold in an auction. So again I went down to city hall, but this time to make sure all the back taxes on the property were paid. Honestly, I was not sure what my grandmother would have done with a "deposit," but we were not going to be on the street just because she hadn't paid the taxes.

Afterward, I let her know what I did, and she dropped the deposit idea. I did all this to take control of my finances. Slowly, I was progressing in decreasing my monthly expenses. I was unemployed, so I qualified for food stamps and Medicaid. Therefore, my food and medical expenses were eliminated. I was now down to $650 of monthly expenses. I had successfully taken control of my finances.

Building a Winning Strategy

Americans are struggling financially. The national credit card balance is nearly **$1 trillion dollars**. However, the problem is not credit cards. It's not knowing your financial profile. We need to take control of our finances. Many of us tend to accumulate as many expenses as we can, almost exceeding our earned income. We love to keep up with the Joneses.

Think about it. When you get a new job or promotion, what do you do? Add more expenses without viewing your personal financial statements. Decide that today is the day you will create and monitor your financial statements to take control of your finances. I walked you through a time when my determination to pursue my dreams forced me to take control of my finances. Now I want to teach you a valuable skill I learned from my first business.

Starting a business was a pivotal moment in my life, and it taught me a lot about finances and the world in general. My financial life became more secure and gave me the idea to run my life the way I would run a profitable business. This was the greatest idea ever! My personal finances mimicked my business finances.

To achieve this, I created financial statements for my personal life. I knew what my expenses were and how much income was coming in. This helped give me a full view of my finances.

In the game of life, financial success often hinges on setting clear goals and implementing a winning strategy to achieve them. Just as a successful business requires careful planning and execution, managing your personal finances effectively means running your life like a profitable enterprise. In this chapter, we'll explore the importance of setting financial goals, crafting a strategic plan, and leveraging key principles to turn your credit card into a valuable asset.

Defining Your Objectives

Just as a business sets objectives to guide its operations and measure success, setting clear financial goals is essential for achieving long-term prosperity. Whether you're saving for a down payment on a home, paying off student loans, building an emergency fund, or investing for retirement, identifying your objectives provide a roadmap for your financial journey.

Creating a Strategic Plan

Once you've established your financial goals, it's time to develop a strategic plan to achieve them. Similar to a business plan outlining objectives, strategies, and tactics, your financial plan should detail how you'll manage your income, expenses, debt, and investments to reach your goals. This plan serves as your playbook for making informed decisions and staying on track despite inevitable challenges.

Leveraging Financial Principles

Just as successful businesses leverage key principles like budgeting, cash flow management, and risk mitigation, incorporating these principles into your personal finances can lead to greater success. By budgeting effectively, optimizing your cash flow, and managing risk through diversification, you can minimize financial stress and maximize your chances of achieving your goals.

Aligning Your Credit Card Strategy

Your credit cards can be powerful tools in your financial arsenal if used strategically. Rather than viewing them as sources of debt, think of them as instruments for achieving your financial objectives. Whether it's earning rewards on everyday purchases, consolidating debt at a lower interest rate, or building credit history for future opportunities, aligning your credit card strategy with your broader financial goals is key to your success.

Tracking Progress and Making Adjustments

Like monitoring key performance indicators in business, tracking your progress toward your financial goals is crucial for success. Regularly review your financial plan, assess your progress, and make adjustments as needed to stay on course. Whether it's increasing savings contributions, cutting expenses, or reallocating investments, being proactive in managing your finances ensures you remain agile and adaptable in pursuit of your objectives.

Setting Spending Goals

To set effective spending goals, it's essential to understand your net income, which is the amount of money you take home after taxes and other deductions. Start by calculating your monthly net income, including all sources of income such as wages, salaries, bonuses, and investment dividends.

Once you have your net income figure, you can create a budget to allocate your income toward various expenses and savings goals. Divide your expenses into categories such as housing, transportation, groceries, utilities, entertainment, and savings. Use historical spending data, receipts, and bills to estimate your monthly expenses accurately.

The 70/20/10 rule is a simple and effective method for managing your finances, helping you allocate your income into three main categories: essential expenses, financial goals, and personal spending. Here's a breakdown of how to use this budgeting rule:

Essential Expenses - 70%

Allocate 70% of your income to cover your essential living expenses. These are the necessary costs that you incur on a regular basis and are required to maintain your basic standard of living.

- **Housing (rent/mortgage)**
- **Utilities (electricity, water, gas)**

- **Groceries**
- **Transportation (car payment, public transit, gas)**
- **Insurance (health, auto, home)**
- **Healthcare (prescriptions, doctor visits)**
- **Minimum Debt Payments (credit cards, loans)**

Financial Goals - 20%

Allocate 20% of your income toward your financial goals. This category focuses on building your future financial security and stability.

- **Savings**
- **Emergency Fund**
- **Investments (stocks, bonds real estate)**
- **Debt Repayment (above minimum payments)**
- **Retirement Fund (401(k), IRA)**

Personal Spending - 10%

Allocate 10% of your income for personal, discretionary spending. These are the non-essential expenses that bring joy and fulfillment to your life.

- **Dining Out**
- **Entertainment (movies, concerts)**
- **Hobbies and Leisure Activities**
- **Travel and Vacations**
- **Personal Care (haircuts, spa treatments)**
- **Shopping (clothing, accessories)**

Adjust these percentages based on your individual circumstances and goals.

Creating a Budget Chart

To visualize your spending goals, create a budget chart that outlines your planned expenses for each category compared to your actual spending. This chart can help you track your progress, identify areas where you may be overspending, and allow you to make adjustments as needed to stay within your budget.

Implementing the 70/20/10 Rule

1. **Assess Your Income:** Calculate your total monthly income after taxes.
2. **Categorize Your Expenses:** List all your expenses and categorize them into essential, financial goals, and personal spending.
3. **Allocate Funds:** Based on the 70/20/10 percentages, allocate your income to each category.,
4. **Track Your Spending:** Monitor your expenses regularly to ensure you stay within the budgeted amounts.
5. **Adjust as Needed:** If you find it difficult to stick to the budget, adjust your allocations while keeping the overall percentages in mind.

The 70/20/10 rule provides a flexible yet disciplined approach to managing your finances, helping you achieve a balance between meeting your immediate needs, securing your future, and enjoying your present. By following this rule, you can take control of your financial life and work toward financial freedom.

Here's an example of a budget chart using the 70/20/10 rule:

Essential Expenses 70%

Expense Category	Amount
Housing	$1,500
Utilities	$300
Groceries	$500
Transportation	$400
Insurance	$300
Healthcare	$200
Minimum Debt Payments	$300
Total	**$3,500**

Financial Goals 20%

Goal Category	Amount
Savings	$400
Emergency Fund	$200
Investments	$200
Debt Repayment	$100
Retirement Fund	$100
Total	**$1,000**

Personal Spending 10%

Spending Category	Amount
Dining Out	$150
Entertainment	$100
Hobbies and Leisure	$100
Travel and Vacations	$50
Personal Care	$50
Shopping	$50
Total	**$500**

By regularly reviewing your budget chart and comparing your actual spending to your planned expenses, you can stay on track with your financial goals and make informed decisions to improve your financial health. Remember, the key to success is being flexible and adaptable, adjusting your budget as needed to accommodate changing circumstances and priorities.

In summary, setting financial goals and creating a strategic plan builds a winning strategy for managing your personal finances. By aligning your credit card strategy with your broader financial objectives and tracking your progress over time, you can turn your credit card into a valuable asset and achieve long-term financial success.

Chapter 5 Questions

1. Why is aligning your credit card strategy with broader financial goals crucial for financial success?

2. How does understanding your net income contribute to effective budgeting and spending goal setting?

3. Discuss the significance of tracking progress and making adjustments to achieve your financial objectives.

4. What role does the 70/20/10 rule play in personal budgeting? How does it help prioritize spending?

5. How can creating a budget chart assist in visualizing spending goals and maintaining financial discipline?

6. Create your own budget using the sample chart below.

Category	Percentage	Planned Amount	Actual Amount	Difference
Essential Expenses	**70%**			
- Housing				
- Utilities				
- Groceries				
- Transportation				
- Insurance				
- Healthcare				
- Minimum Debt Payments				
Financial Goals	**20%**			
- Savings				
- Emergency Fund				
- Investments				
- Debt Repayment				
- Retirement Fund				
Personal Spending	**10%**			
- Dining Out				
- Entertainment				
- Hobbies and Leisure				
- Travel and Vacations				
- Personal Care				
- Shopping				

Total Income: [Your Net Income]

CHAPTER 6

CHOOSING THE RIGHT
CREDIT CARD: PLAYING OFFENSE

Choosing the right credit card is not just about swiping; it's about strategically aligning your financial goals with the card's perks and benefits, transforming everyday spending into an asset.

—Dr. Charley Thomas

It's the end of my first year in pharmacy school, and I am feeling fantastic. I had a successful year and even made the Dean's List each semester. It was a wonderful feeling. I am in the midst of accomplishing my goal. I'm still following my budget and wanted to celebrate by attending the end-of-year pharmacy party at Metro. I met a few friends there, and we partied, just having a great time. I decided to celebrate by getting myself a drink. While waiting at the bar, I heard a voice beside me saying, "You buying your own drink?"

"Yes," I replied.

"Nah, I got it. What's your name?" he asked.

"Charley," I replied.

From that moment on, we were inseparable. As our relationship started to blossom, he began to notice I was keeping a tight budget and not buying myself anything. He offered to buy me some clothes, and boy, was I offended. I didn't know how to process that, because I was proud of how I was keeping to my budget. But now I was embarrassed, and it made me feel a certain way about myself. I was okay with missing out on events and not living the life of a woman in her early twenties. Instead, I focused on being a great mom and breaking generational curses. So, just having him mention that triggered something inside of me.

Eventually, we had a talk, and I opened up about everything. I finally put my pride aside and accepted his offer. I'm glad I did because I was able to breathe a little and enjoy life. I was gaining a different perspective on life in the VIP lane, and I loved it! From that moment on, I knew that's how I wanted to live my life.

I remember one of the trips we took to Vegas; it was epic. It was a guy's trip, but after being out there for a half day, he flew me to Vegas because he was missing my presence. He had everything planned with top-notch service for my arrival. When I arrived, he had a car waiting for me. I also received flowers at the hotel.

He reserved a big two-bedroom suite with a wraparound balcony with a fantastic view. This was the beginning of my love for travel. Everything was VIP treatment, no standing in lines, and I met some amazing people. My life was poppin', but it was poppin' because of his lifestyle. I thought, *Now I know what it's like to have happiness in my life, to be surrounded by positivity.*

But soon, I realized that my happiness wasn't within. I was living the glamorous life of star athletes and celebrities but losing focus on my goals. I was even on the verge of failing a class in pharmacy school. That hurt my soul.

Self-discovery is an ongoing process. Most people experience some level of self-discovery at different points in their lives, starting as teens. I didn't have the opportunity to go through any of those moments as an adolescent because I was so busy making changes and providing a good life for my son. School and parenting consumed my life until I met my then-boyfriend. Shortly after, I added being a great girlfriend to the list.

Never once did I try to figure out what my interests were. It took me some years after we split to do my own introspection. As I progressed in my career and created different income streams, my time was freed. This allowed me to carve out time for self-care, explore new activities, seek support, set goals, and prioritize my own needs. I rediscovered my interest in travel and how it makes me happy. I now have happiness within.

Discovering my love for travel helped me choose the credit card that would best benefit my travel desires with little to no cost to me.

Choosing the Right Card for You

Choosing the right credit card can be intimidating, especially when considering the vast number of options available in the market. However, choosing the right credit card is crucial, as it can help you save money, earn rewards, and build your credit score.

Steps for choosing the right card:

Step 1. Determine the Purpose of the Credit Card

Decide on the purpose of the credit card, whether it is for everyday purchases, travel, or building credit. This can help you narrow down your options and select a card that suits your needs.

Step 2. Review Your Credit Score and Credit History

Your credit score and credit history play a crucial role in determining the type of credit card you can qualify for. Most credit card issuers require a minimum credit score to be eligible for their credit cards. Therefore, knowing your credit score before applying for a credit card is essential. You can obtain your credit score for free from a credit bureau (Equifax, TransUnion, or Experian).

You should also review your credit history and ensure there are no errors in your credit report. A good credit history and score can help you qualify for the best credit card offers, including those with low-interest rates and generous rewards.

Step 3. Identify Your Spending Habits and Needs

To choose the right credit card, you must identify your spending habits and needs. Consider the categories where you spend the most, such as gas, groceries, dining out, travel, etc. Look for credit cards that offer rewards and benefits in these categories.

For instance, if you frequently travel, you may want to consider a travel rewards credit card that offers rewards points or miles for every dollar spent on travel-related expenses. If you frequently dine out, a credit card offering cash back or rewards points for dining purchases may be your best option.

Step 4. Understand the Different Types of Credit Cards

Credit cards come in different types, each with benefits and drawbacks. Understanding the different types of credit cards and their features is essential to choosing the right credit card for you. Here are some of the most common types of credit cards:

Rewards	Cash back	Business
Travel	Secured	Co-branded
Balance Transfer	Student	Store

Rewards

Rewards credit cards offer rewards points or cash back for every dollar spent on purchases. These rewards can be redeemed for merchandise, travel, gift cards, and statement credits. Rewards credit cards may come with an annual fee, and the rewards program may have restrictions and limitations.

Travel

Travel credit cards are designed specifically for individuals who frequently travel for leisure or business. These cards offer rewards and benefits tailored to travelers, such as earning points or miles for every dollar spent on travel-related purchases, including flights, hotels, car rentals, and dining. Travel credit cards often come with additional perks like travel insurance, airport lounge access, free checked bags, and no foreign transaction fees, making them highly valuable for those who spend a significant amount of time on the road or in the air. By using a travel credit card wisely, cardholders can accumulate points or miles that can be redeemed for free or discounted travel, ultimately enhancing your travel experiences and saving money.

Balance Transfer

Balance transfer credit cards allow you to transfer high-interest credit card balances to a card with a lower interest rate. These cards often come with a 0% APR introductory period for balance transfers but may charge a balance transfer fee. After the introductory period, the interest rate may increase significantly.

Cash Back

Cash back credit cards offer cash back for every dollar spent on purchases. These cards may have different cash back rates for different categories, such as gas, groceries, dining, etc. Cash back credit cards may also come with an annual fee.

Secured

Secured credit cards require a security deposit to be placed with the credit card issuer. The credit limit is usually equal to the amount of the security deposit. Secured credit cards are often used to build or rebuild credit.

Student

Student credit cards are designed for college students with limited credit histories. These cards often come with lower credit limits and higher interest rates but may offer rewards and other benefits.

Business

Business credit cards are designed specifically for businesses to manage their expenses. They function like personal credit cards but are tailored to meet the unique needs of businesses, such as helping them keep track of expenses, earn rewards, and manage employee spending.

Co-branded Credit Cards

Co-branded credit cards are issued in partnership between a credit card company and a specific brand or retailer. These cards offer rewards and benefits that are tailored to the brand's products and services. For example, an airline co-branded credit card might provide extra miles for purchases made with the airline, priority boarding, and discounts on in-flight purchases. Similarly, a hotel chain co-branded credit card might offer free nights, room upgrades, and points for every dollar spent at the hotel's properties. Co-branded credit cards are an excellent choice for loyal customers of a particular brand, as they can maximize their rewards and take advantage of exclusive perks and discounts offered by the partner brand.

Store Credit Cards

Store credit cards are issued by retail stores and are intended for use primarily at the issuing store or its affiliated brands. These cards often come with benefits such as discounts on purchases, special financing offers, and rewards points that can be redeemed for store merchandise. Store credit cards can be either closed-loop, meaning they can only be used at the issuing store, or open-loop, which can be used anywhere that accepts major credit cards like Visa or Mastercard. While store credit cards can be a great way to save money and earn rewards at your favorite retailers, it's important to be mindful of their typically higher interest rates and the potential to overspend due to the attractive discounts and promotions.

Step 5. Compare Credit Card Offers

Once you have identified your spending habits and needs and have an understanding of the different types of credit cards, it is time to compare credit card offers. Look for credit cards that offer rewards or benefits that align with your spending habits and needs.

Comparing credit card offers and selecting the best one for your needs can seem overwhelming. Here are some key factors to consider when comparing credit card offers and choosing the best one:

Annual fees	Other benefits
Interest rates	Other fees
Rewards programs	

Annual Fees

Check for annual fees and compare them across the cards. Make sure that any rewards or benefits offered justify the annual fee. Note that if you are building your credit, you should not get a card with an annual fee.

Interest Rates

Look at each card's interest rates (APRs) and consider whether you plan to carry a balance or pay off your balance in full each month. If you plan to carry a balance, look for a card with a lower interest rate.

Rewards Programs

Compare rewards programs across cards, including earning rates, redemption options, and any sign-up bonuses. Consider whether the rewards offered match your spending habits and whether you can easily redeem rewards for things you need.

Other Benefits

Look at other benefits offered by each card, such as travel insurance, extended warranty coverage, purchase protection, and concierge services.

Other Fees

Compare other fees, such as late payment fees, foreign transaction fees, and balance transfer fees, to ensure you know what costs are involved.

Once you have compared these factors across different credit cards, it's time to decide which card works best for you. Consider your spending habits, financial goals, and any specific rewards or benefits that are important to you. While most people don't do this, read the terms and conditions carefully before applying for the card to be certain you fully understand its features and fees.

Step 6. Consider sign-up bonuses

Many credit cards offer sign-up bonuses, such as cash back or points for new cardholders. Evaluate these bonuses and consider how they align with your spending habits and financial goals.

Step 7. Read the fine print

Before applying for a credit card, make sure to read the terms and conditions carefully. Pay attention to the interest rate, fees, rewards, and other policies. This can help you avoid any surprises later on.

By following these steps, you can choose a credit card that aligns with your spending habits and financial goals. You can maximize the benefits of your credit card and avoid unnecessary fees and charges.

Choosing the right credit card: A Family's Real Life Approach

Meet the Thompsons, a family of three consisting of Mark, Emily, and their teenage daughter, Lily. As they navigated the complexities of modern life, they realized the need for a reliable credit card to manage their expenses efficiently and earn rewards along the way. Let's see how the Thompsons used the steps to choose the right credit card.

Step 1: Determining the Purpose

Mark and Emily Thompson sat down one evening to discuss their financial goals and the purpose of obtaining a credit card. They wanted a card that would help cover their everyday expenses and provide benefits like cash back or travel rewards to enhance their family experiences.

Step 2: Reviewing Credit Score and History

Curious about their creditworthiness, Mark and Emily decided to check their credit scores and credit histories online. While Mark had an excellent credit score due to his responsible credit card use in the past, Emily's score was lower than expected; she'd missed a payment on a utility bill a few months ago.

Step 3: Identifying Spending Habits and Needs

With Lily entering her teenage years, the Thompsons anticipated an increase in their expenses, particularly in categories like groceries, entertainment, and family outings. They wanted a credit card that would reward them for these everyday purchases while offering additional perks like extended warranties or purchase protection.

Step 4: Understanding Different Types of Credit Cards

Mark and Emily took the time to research the different types of credit cards available, including cashback cards, travel rewards cards, and cards with low introductory APR offers. They learned the pros and cons of each and considered how they aligned with their family's lifestyle and spending habits.

Step 5: Comparing Credit Card Offers

Armed with knowledge, the Thompsons began comparing credit card offers from various issuers. They looked for cards with no annual fees, competitive rewards programs, and flexible redemption options. Additionally, they considered cards that offered bonus rewards on categories like groceries, dining, and gas stations—areas where they spent the most.

Step 6: Considering the Sign-Up Bonus

One credit card offer caught Mark's attention—a travel rewards card with a generous sign-up bonus of 60,000 miles after spending $4,000 in the first three months. Intrigued by the possibility of earning free flights and hotel stays for their next family vacation, Mark and Emily carefully evaluated the offer's terms and conditions.

Step 7: Reading the Fine Print

Before making a final decision, Mark and Emily made sure to read the fine print of the credit card agreement. They paid close attention to details such as interest rates, balance transfer fees, foreign transaction fees, and any restrictions on rewards redemption. They also reviewed the card's benefits, including travel insurance and purchase protection, to ensure they understood the full value proposition.

After much deliberation and discussion, the Thompsons chose a travel rewards credit card that offered a competitive sign-up bonus, generous rewards on everyday purchases, and valuable travel benefits. With their new card in hand, they felt confident in their ability to manage their finances responsibly while enjoying the perks and rewards that came with it.

Chapter 6 Questions

1. Why is it important to choose the right credit card?

2. How can understanding your spending habits help you select the most beneficial type of credit card?

3. What are the common types of credit cards?

4. Why is it important to read the terms and conditions before applying for a credit card?

5. When comparing and choosing credit card offers, which key factors will help you make an informed decision?

CHAPTER 7

CREDIT CARD REWARDS: PLAYING OFFENSE

Maximizing your credit card rewards is not just about earning points; it's about turning everyday purchases into opportunities for savings and financial growth

—Dr. Charley Thomas

During my self-discovery, I found inner peace and happiness. Also, I learned I genuinely love to travel. Through travel, I can broaden my horizons, challenge my perspectives, and create lasting memories. I truly believe I suffered from PTSD from all the trauma I had experienced. Traveling helped me heal.

Choosing the right credit card also helped enhance my lifestyle and made my life more fulfilling with little to no cost to me. I travel at least once per quarter, with one of my trips being international. One year I decided to spend my birthday in a place that's considered heaven on earth—Bali, Indonesia.

Indonesia is located in the southern hemisphere of Southeast Asia and shares land borders with Malaysia, Papua New Guinea, and East Timor-Leste. It is an archipelago country consisting of more than 17,000 islands located between the Indian Ocean and the Pacific Ocean. It is also the world's largest island country and spans a vast area from Sumatra in the west to Papua in the east. While the western part of Indonesia is located in Southeast Asia, the eastern part is closer to the continent of Australia. As you can imagine, traveling from the United States will be quite a long trip.

In Chapter Five, we learned to take control of our finances and run our lives like a profitable business. Therefore, I will make sure the trip expenses align with my financial statements. Then I will research how current credit card rewards will help eliminate some, if not the total cost.

When I travel, I like accommodations at locations unique to that area. Therefore, my expenses are slightly higher than the average cost. Knowing that, I started my research.

For my trip to Bali, I wanted to stay in two different areas of the island to maximize my time. For my first accommodation, I decided I wanted a view like no other—from the top of cliffs overlooking the Indian Ocean. I wanted that feeling of being on the edge of the world, and I found the perfect location. Also, I wanted to disconnect from the world and reconnect with myself and nature. That brings me to my second accommodation: adults-only treehouse-type villas that offered the "Naked Experience." There were no doors or walls, and it was perfect. I was about to surround myself with endless layers of nature with beautiful views of the Balinese jungle and mountain peaks.

I found two locations and the cost to include in my budget. I did not focus on flights first because I knew I had 123,000 miles with

Delta Airlines and over 100,000 in reward points on my Regions Credit Card. This meant my miles and/or rewards would cover my flight expenses. Just like that, my credit card use decreased my travel expenses.

However, just because I have miles and rewards doesn't mean I want to use them all. So, I still researched the cheapest flights. The flight was twenty-three hours one way with a four-hour layover in Taipei, Taiwan. To make the best of my time, I like to have access to airport lounges. Currently, I only had access to Delta lounges, but I was flying China Airlines. However, I did not want to add any other expenses to my vacation budget. So, I decided to search for a travel credit card.

In Chapter One, we learned to understand our motives for applying for a credit card. Before applying, I asked myself the following questions:

1. **Why am I getting this credit card?**
   I was getting the credit card to benefit from the travel perks. For example, complimentary airport lounge access, global entry credit, and better prices for hotel accommodations.

2. **What's my credit card's purpose?**
   My credit card's purpose was to get exclusive deals and access for travel.

3. **How will it impact me?**
   I had already created a budget and could afford the trip without using my credit card; therefore, paying the balance in full was not a problem. I did not plan to purchase or

make any big investments until the last quarter of the year. So, this will improve my credit score and help with lower interest rates and terms for real estate.

As I previously shared in Chapter Five, I already had my finances under control. Next, I needed to choose the right credit card, the skill learned in Chapter Six. I compared many travel credit cards and ended up with two contenders, Chase Sapphire Reserve and American Express Platinum Card. I knew my odds of approval for either card were great based on my credit history and credit score.

Both cards have an annual fee and offer many travel perks with a sign-on bonus. I ended up applying for the Chase Sapphire Reserve over the American Express Platinum Credit Card because it aligned with my spending habits for the next three months, and the benefits outweighed the annual fee.

Let's check out the offers and how I used the card within the first ten days to get the bonus offer, without paying out of pocket for the annual fee and maximizing my rewards.

Chase Sapphire Reserve Offer: Annual fee of $550

- 60,000 bonus points after spending $4,000 in the first three months from account opening (This is $900 toward travel.)
- $300 annual travel credit applied to statement
- 10x total points on hotels and car rentals purchased through Chase Ultimate Rewards
- 5x total points on flights purchased through Chase Ultimate Rewards

- 10x total points on Chase Dining purchased through Chase Ultimate Rewards
- 3x points on other dining
- 1x points on all other purchases
- 50% more redemption value
- Complimentary airport lounge access
- Global Entry or TSA PreCheck fee credit
- The Luxury Hotel & Resort Collection (complimentary room upgrades and daily breakfast at certain properties.)
- Lyft discounts and priority
- DoorDash premium subscription
- Instacart premium subscription
- Trip cancellation/interruption insurance
- Auto rental collision damage waiver
- Lost luggage reimbursement
- Trip delay reimbursement
- Emergency evacuation and transportation

The long list of rewards demonstrates that this card was the perfect credit card for me. Yay! Now, let's learn how I maximized the perks and quickly turned this credit card into an asset.

I purchased my accommodations for my Bali vacation through the Chase Ultimate Rewards portal. I earned 10x points, spent over $4,000 to get the 60,000 bonus points, and received the $300 travel credit. I applied for a Global Entry to save time during arrival. Both hotels are part of the Luxury Hotel & Resort Collection, so I received a complimentary room upgrade with daily breakfast. I activated the Lyft premium subscription to get a discounted and priority ride to and from the airport. I now have complimentary airport lounge access, which will give me comfort during this long travel and four-hour layover. In addition, I now have trip cancellation/interruption insurance just in case something happens at no cost to me.

Here's a table of the general costs for my Bali trip and how much I paid after maximizing my rewards:

BALI TRIP EXPENSES		
	Original cost	Actual out-of-pocket cost
Villa 1	$4,260	$2,154
Villa 2	$3,152	$2,217
Flights	$3,100	$21
Airport Travel	$200	$70
Global Entry	$100	$0
Airport Lounge Membership	$249	$0
Total	$10,961	$4,465

Following the steps in Chapters One through Six helped me choose the perfect credit card, maximizing my rewards based on my spending habits and decreasing my expenses to enjoy a wonderful vacation at a fraction of the original cost.

Credit card issuers offer reward programs to stay competitive and get us to apply. I showed you how I maximize my rewards using points. Now, let's learn how to unlock its benefits.

Unlocking the Benefits

Credit cards are a convenient payment method that offer consumers a wide range of benefits. One of the most popular benefits of credit cards is the rewards program, which can provide cash back, points, or miles.

Cash Back Rewards

Cash back rewards are one of the simplest and most popular types of rewards programs. In a survey, 41% of users chose cash back as their favorite rewards program from credit cards. With cash back rewards, a percentage of your purchase amount is returned to you in the form of cash or a credit to your account. The percentage of cash back varies depending on the card, type of purchase, and the specific rewards program. Most cards offer anywhere from 1% - 5% cash back.

To earn more cash back rewards, we can use merchant category codes (MCCs), which categorize the type of merchant for each transaction. By understanding how MCCs work, you may earn more cash back rewards on your credit card purchases.

Here are some ways to earn more cash back using MCCs:

Choose a credit card with bonus categories

Many credit cards offer bonus cash back rewards for purchases made at specific merchant categories. For example, some cards offer higher cash back rewards for purchases made at grocery stores, gas stations, restaurants, or travel-related expenses. Make sure to choose a credit card that offers bonus categories that align with your spending habits.

Pay attention to merchant categories

Be aware of which MCCs are associated with the merchants where you make purchases. For example, some stores that sell groceries and other items may not be categorized as grocery stores by your credit card company. In this case, you may not earn the bonus cash back reward for grocery store purchases. Check with your credit card company to confirm which MCCs are associated with your preferred merchants.

Use multiple cards for different categories

If you have multiple credit cards with bonus categories, consider using the card with the highest cash back rewards for each category. For example, use one card for grocery store purchases and another for gas station purchases. This strategy can help you maximize your cash back rewards.

Shop through online portals

Some credit card companies offer additional cash back rewards when you shop at certain merchants through their online shopping portals. Make sure to check your credit card company's website to see if they offer this benefit and which merchants are eligible.

To earn more cash back using merchant category codes, choose a credit card with bonus categories, pay attention to merchant categories, use multiple cards for different categories, and shop through online portals. By following these strategies, you can maximize your cash back rewards on credit card purchases.

Reward Points

Reward points are another popular type of rewards program. With reward points, you earn points for purchases made with the card, which can then be redeemed for various rewards, such as travel expenses, cash, gift cards, or merchandise. The value of credit card points can vary depending on the credit card rewards program and the redemption options available.

Generally, credit card points can be worth anywhere from 0.5 to 2 cents per point, but some programs may offer more or less value. This is why choosing the right credit card is important. We should be looking for credit cards that offer more value for the points. For example, 10 times, 5 times, or 3 times the points on purchases in specific categories. That way, if you decide to cash in on the rewards, you are getting more value than the cash back option.

This is why I prefer reward points over cash back. We'll receive a greater return on the money we are already spending. For example, if a credit card rewards program offers 10 points per dollar spent, and each point is worth 1 cent, then we would be earning 10% cash back on our purchases.

If the program offers travel rewards, the value of the points can vary depending on the airline or hotel partner where you choose to redeem your points. In some cases, you may get more value out of your points by transferring them to a travel partner or redeeming them for travel-related purchases, such as flights or hotel stays. Like with my Chase Sapphire Reserve credit card, I receive 50% more redemption value for travel through the Chase Ultimate Rewards. (For example, 60,000 points are worth $900, so that's 22.5% cash back.)

It's important to read the terms and conditions of your credit card rewards program and understand the redemption options available to ensure you get the most value out of your points. This is one of my favorite reward programs for its unlimited benefits. At the beginning of this chapter, I gave you a real-life example of how I used the reward points to my benefit. To do this, you must know the value of the points.

Miles Rewards

Miles rewards programs are popular with travelers, as they offer miles that can be redeemed for flights, upgrades, hotels, rental cars, and other travel-related expenses. Miles rewards programs work similarly to points rewards programs, with miles earned for purchases made with the card. Some programs also offer additional benefits such as priority boarding, lounge access, and free checked bags. Look for credit cards that offer high-mile rewards for purchases you make regularly. Some cards also offer bonus miles for signing up or for spending a certain amount in the first few months.

Airlines offer frequent flier or loyalty programs that accumulate miles to reward customers for their loyalty and encourage them to continue using their services. Do *not* get this confused with your credit card miles reward program. These are separate and can be used to your advantage to maximize your benefits.

For example, I am a frequent flier with Delta Airlines and have a SkyMiles account. For each flight I take, I receive miles via the loyalty program. I also have a credit card with a rewards program in which I redeem my flight rewards. By using this method, I paid $0 for my flight and gained miles via the loyalty program. This got me closer to the Delta loyalty status that allows free upgrades, priority boarding, and more miles. You see how strategically that came full circle?

It's important to note that these programs often have restrictions and blackout dates, so make sure to read the terms and conditions carefully before signing up. Additionally, miles and points usually have an expiration date, so make sure you use them before they expire.

Maximizing Credit Card Rewards

Maximizing your credit card rewards requires more than just accumulating points or miles; it involves a strategic approach to redeeming those rewards, taking advantage of promotional offers, and managing annual fees. By understanding how to effectively navigate these aspects, you can significantly enhance the value you get from your credit cards, turning everyday purchases into opportunities for substantial savings and exclusive benefits.

Strategically redeeming rewards

Choose the best time to redeem your rewards for maximum value. For example, redeeming points for travel can often offer more value than redeeming them for cash back.

Special promotions

Credit card companies often offer special promotions or bonus categories that can help you earn extra rewards. Keep an eye out for these promotions and take advantage of them when they align with your spending habits.

Annual fees

Some credit cards charge annual fees, which can eat into your rewards. Make sure to factor in the annual fee when evaluating the overall value of the rewards and benefits of a credit card. Many credit cards with great reward programs do not require an annual fee.

If you are using a credit card to build your credit or just starting out with credit cards, avoid annual fee cards. I only recommend getting an annual fee credit card if you are experienced with maximizing the benefits of your credit card. I have a total of six personal credit cards, and only one has an annual fee. I just recently decided to get it because the benefits justified the fee, and I ended up not paying for it out of my budget.

By understanding how different rewards programs operate, selecting the right credit card based on your spending patterns, and staying up-to-date with special promotions and redemption options, you can turn your everyday expenses into valuable opportunities for significant savings. The key is to approach your credit card use with intention, discipline, and a well-thought-out strategy. This way, your credit card becomes a powerful tool that works for you, not against you, turning your credit card game into a winning strategy.

Chapter 7 Questions

1. What are the three common reward programs?

2. How can having multiple credit cards with different reward categories maximize your benefits?

3. Explain the role of Merchant Category Codes (MCC) in maximizing your cash back rewards.

4. What strategies can you use to earn more cash back rewards by leveraging MCCs and credit card bonus categories?

5. Why is it important to understand the redemption options for your credit -card rewards to maximize their value?

CHAPTER 8

CREDIT CARD DEBT MANAGEMENT: PLAYING TO WIN

*According to a 2023 survey conducted by Payroll. org, **78%** of adults live paycheck to paycheck. **Three out of five** adults don't keep a budget, and two out of three families don't have an emergency fund. This simply means that most people are struggling with financial literacy. And it's part of why we get into credit card debt.*

—Dr. Charley Thomas

At 5:00 a.m. on a Wednesday, a notification sounded as I was heading to the gym for my routine workout. A client sent me an email for a consultation. Immediately, I knew some financial issue was pressing. So, I scheduled a meeting for 10:00 am that same day.

The meeting was about helping my client manage her credit card debt and creating a plan to get out of the rat race. My first question was, *"Do you know where you stand financially right now?"*

"What exactly do you mean?" she asked,

"Are you aware of your current income, expenses, debts, assets, and liabilities?" I replied. This is the first question I ask because most people are not aware of where they stand financially. I know this personally because I have been there. Her answer was, *"No."*

Seventy-eight percent of adults live paycheck to paycheck. **Three out of five** adults don't keep a budget, and two out of three families don't have an emergency fund. Most of us are struggling with financial literacy, and it's partly why we get into credit card debt.

We all want to live the American Dream by purchasing real estate, and my client had done just that. She purchased a beautiful home and used her savings for the down payment. The cost that blindsided her was the closing cost, which depleted her savings. So she used her credit cards to offset some of the extra expenses. The first problem my client suffered is being unaware of where she stood financially, which is the most critical.

Why is this so important?

Knowing where you stand financially means clearly understanding your current financial situation. This includes having knowledge of your income (net and gross), expenses, debts, assets, and liabilities.

To know where you stand financially, start by creating a budget that tracks your income and expenses. In Chapter Five, we learned how to take control of our finances by running our lives like a profitable business. This will help you identify areas where you can cut back on expenses and potentially increase your savings.

It's also important to take stock of your debts, including any loans or credit card balances, and make a plan to pay them off. Additionally, you should be aware of your assets, such as savings accounts, retirement accounts, and investments, as well as any liabilities, such as mortgages or car payments.

A clear understanding of your financial situation can help you make informed decisions about your spending, savings, and investing. It can also help you identify areas where you may need to make changes to improve your financial health and achieve your long-term financial goals.

So, back to my client's story. After her consultation, her first assignment was to create a personal financial statement.

During our following meeting, we reviewed her financial statements and identified areas for improvement. Her next step was to fill out the credit card template, which helped her understand the terms of her credit cards. She listed her current APR, fees, terms, reward program perks, and the amounts she owed on each card. This allowed us to calculate the interest being paid on each card.

We then assessed her current credit score and history to determine the best option to manage her credit card debt. Based on that data, a balance transfer was the best option. I helped her choose the perfect balance transfer credit card, with an offer for 18 months with zero percent APR. We worked on a budget and plan to eliminate her credit card debt in 15 months.

My client had not thought twice about offsetting her expenses by using her credit card after purchasing a home. If she had known she would be paying for that financial decision for years, she would not have charged the expenses and would have created a spending plan from the beginning. It is easy to get into debt but hard to get out of it.

Understanding the Debt Cycle

A debt cycle is a recurring pattern of borrowing, spending, and repayment that can create a self-perpetuating cycle of debt. Debt can be a useful tool for achieving financial goals, such as buying a home or pursuing an education. However, when debt is not managed properly, it can become a vicious cycle and difficult to break free. Credit card debt is the most common form of debt, and the high-interest rates make it challenging to pay off.

Credit card debt can quickly spiral out of control if we do not take steps to manage it. Every month we carry a balance on our credit card we accrue interest, which makes paying off the debt more difficult.

Breaking the Debt Cycle

Breaking the debt cycle requires financial discipline, strategic planning, and commitment. **The best way to accomplish that is by doing the following:**

Assess your debt
Create a debt repayment program
Negotiate with your credit card issuer
Consider balance transfers

Assess your debt

The first step in breaking the debt cycle is to assess your current financial situation. This includes taking stock of all your debt, including credit card balances, loans, and other forms of debt.

To assess your credit card debt, you'll need to gather all your credit card information, including the balances, interest rates, and minimum payments. Once you have a complete picture of your debt, you can begin to develop a plan for paying it off.

Create a debt repayment plan

To pay off your credit card debt, you'll need to create a repayment plan that works for your budget and financial goals.

Managing and eliminating debt is a critical step toward achieving financial stability and freedom. A well-structured debt repayment plan can help you systematically reduce and eventually eliminate your debt. **Here's a step-by-step guide to creating an effective debt repayment plan:**

Step 1: List all your debts

Start by making a comprehensive list of all your debts and include the following details:

Creditor name
Total amount owed
Interest rate
Minimum monthly payment
Due date

Step 2: Calculate your total debt

Add up the total amount of all your debts. This will give you a clear picture of how much you owe in total and help you set realistic repayment goals.

Step 3: Choose a repayment strategy

There are two popular strategies for debt repayment: the **Debt Snowball** and the **Debt Avalanche** methods.

Debt Snowball Method: Focus on paying off your smallest debt first while making minimum payments on all other debts. Once the smallest debt is paid off, move to the next smallest, and so on. This method provides quick wins and can be motivating.

Debt Avalanche Method: Focus on paying off the debt with the highest interest rate first while making minimum payments on all other debts. Once the highest interest debt is paid off, move to the next highest, and so on. This method saves the most money on interest in the long run.

Choose the method that best fits your financial situation and personal preference.

Step 4: Create a budget

Establish a monthly budget to ensure you have enough money to cover your debt payments and other essential expenses. Allocate as much as possible toward your debt repayment while maintaining a reasonable lifestyle. Use the 70/20/10 rule as a guideline, dedicating 20% of your income toward your financial goals, including debt repayment.

Step 5: Increase your income and reduce expenses

Look for opportunities to increase your income, such as taking on a side job, freelancing, or selling unused items. Additionally, reduce unnecessary expenses to free up more money for debt repayment. Every extra dollar you can put toward your debt will help you pay it off faster.

Step 6: Make extra payments whenever possible

Whenever you receive extra income, such as a tax refund, bonus, or gift, apply it toward your debt. Extra payments can significantly reduce the principal amount you owe, leading to less interest accrued and a faster payoff.

Step 7: Monitor your progress

Regularly review your progress to stay motivated and make adjustments as needed. Track how much you've paid off and how much closer you are to being debt-free. Celebrate your milestones along the way to keep your momentum going.

Step 8: Avoid accumulating new debt

While you're working on paying off your existing debt, avoid accumulating new debt. Be mindful of your spending and use credit cards responsibly, ensuring you pay off the balance in full each month to avoid interest charges.

Sample Debt Repayment Plan

Here's an example of how a debt repayment plan might look using the Debt Avalanche Method:

Total Monthly Income: $3,000
Essential Expenses (70%): $2,100
Financial Goals (20%): $600

Debt Repayment: $500
Savings: $100

Personal Spending (10%): $300

Debt Details:

Debts	Balance	Interest	Minimum Payment
Credit Card A	$1,000	18%	$25
Credit Card B	$3,000	12%	$75
Student Loan	$5,000	6%	$50

Debt Avalanche Plan:
1. Pay minimum payments on Credit Card B and Student Loan.
2. Allocate $400 toward Credit Card A (minimum payment of $25 + extra $375).
3. Once Credit Card A is paid off, allocate $400 toward Credit Card B (minimum payment of $75 + extra $325).

> 4. Once Credit Card B is paid off, allocate $400 toward Student Loan (minimum payment of $50 + extra $350).
>
> By following this plan, you'll systematically reduce your debt, starting with the highest interest rate, and ultimately achieve financial freedom. Remember, the key to success is consistency and dedication. Stay focused, and you'll be debt-free before you know it.

Negotiate with your credit card issuer

If you're having trouble making your payments, consider reaching out to your credit card issuer to negotiate a lower interest rate or a payment plan that works for you. Most credit card issuers have credit card hardship programs.

Consider balance transfers

A balance transfer can be an effective strategy to reduce interest charges and pay off debt faster. Transferring high-interest credit card debt to a card with a lower interest rate can save you money and simplify your payments. **Here's a step-by-step guide to performing a balance transfer:**

> ### Step 1: Assess Your Debt and Credit Score
> Start by reviewing all your current credit card balances, interest rates, and minimum payments. Additionally, check your credit score to understand your eligibility for balance transfer offers. A higher credit score increases your chances of getting approved for cards with favorable terms.

Step 2: Research Balance Transfer Credit Cards

Look for credit cards that offer low or 0% introductory APR on balance transfers. Pay attention to the length of the introductory period, the regular APR after the introductory period ends, and any balance transfer fees (typically 3-5% of the amount transferred).

Step 3: Calculate Potential Savings

Determine how much you could save by transferring your balances. Compare the interest you're currently paying with the interest you'd pay with the new card, including any transfer fees. Use online balance transfer calculators to help with this comparison.

Step 4: Apply for a Balance Transfer Credit Card

Once you've identified a suitable balance transfer card, apply for it. Be prepared to provide personal information, financial details, and information about the balances you wish to transfer. Approval usually depends on your credit score and income.

Step 5: Initiate the Balance Transfer

After approval, follow the issuer's instructions to initiate the balance transfer. You'll need to provide information about the existing credit card accounts and the amount you wish to transfer. This process can take anywhere from a few days to a few weeks, so continue making payments on your old cards until the transfer is complete.

Step 6: Monitor the Transfer and Pay Off Your Debt

Keep an eye on your accounts to ensure the balances are transferred correctly. Once the transfer is complete, focus on paying off the transferred balance within the introductory period to avoid interest charges. Set up automatic payments or reminders to ensure you don't miss any payments.

Step 7: Avoid New Debt

While paying off your transferred balance, avoid accumulating new debt. Resist the temptation to use the old credit cards and focus on reducing your overall debt.

Step 8: Review Terms and Conditions

Carefully read the terms and conditions of your new credit card to understand any fees, penalties, or changes in interest rates that could affect you. This will help you avoid unexpected charges and make the most of your balance transfer.

Step 9: Create a Debt Repayment Plan

Develop a plan to pay off your transferred balance within the introductory period. Allocate as much as possible toward your monthly payments and consider using the 70/20/10 budgeting rule to manage your finances effectively.

Example:

Current Credit Card	Balance Transfer Credit Card
Balance: $5,000	Introductory APR: 0% for 12 months
Interest Rate: 18%	Balance Transfer Fee: 3%
Monthly Payment: $150	Regular APR: 15% after 12 months

1. **Calculate Transfer Fee:** 3% of $5,000 = $150
2. **Total Balance Transferred:** $5,000 + $150 = $5,150

3. **Monthly Payment Needed to Pay Off in 12 Months:**
$5,150 / 12 = $429.17

By transferring the balance and paying $429.17 each month, you can pay off the debt within the 12-month introductory period without incurring additional interest. This saves you significant interest charges compared to continuing with the 18% APR on the original card.

Credit card debt can feel overwhelming, but with the right approach you have the power to take control and turn the situation around. Knowing where you stand financially is the first step toward gaining that control. By creating a solid debt repayment plan, negotiating better terms with your credit card issuers, and using tools like balance transfers wisely, you can break free from the debt cycle and build a more secure financial future. Remember, the journey to financial freedom isn't about quick fixes—it's about making consistent, informed decisions that lead to lasting results. Stay committed, stay focused, and remember that every step you take brings you closer to winning the credit card game and achieving the peace of mind you deserve. You've got this!

Chapter 8 Questions

1. What does "knowing where you stand financially" mean, and why is it important?

2. What is a budget, and how can it help you manage credit card debt?

3. What are the two most common methods for prioritizing debt repayment, and how do they differ?

4. How can a balance transfer help reduce credit card debt, and what steps should you take to perform one effectively?

5. Why is it important to avoid accumulating new debt while paying off existing credit card balances?

6. What role does financial discipline play in breaking the debt cycle and achieving financial freedom?

CHAPTER 9

MAXIMIZING CREDIT CARD REWARDS: ADVANCED TRAVEL HACKING STRATEGIES

The smartest way to spend is by earning rewards with intention—turning everyday purchases into extraordinary experiences.

–Dr. Charley Thomas

What if I told you that your daily expenses like groceries, gas, and utilities could get you a free vacation to Europe? No, it's not a pipe dream; it's a reality that you can achieve by applying some advanced travel hacking techniques. Imagine booking your dream vacation to Europe, but instead of charging the entire trip to your credit card, you use the points and rewards you've accumulated over time. The flights are free, excluding taxes, and the hotel stay is nearly free. Your only expense will be food and souvenirs.

That's the magic of strategic credit card usage—it's not just about earning rewards; it's about using them wisely to make life's biggest adventures more affordable. In Chapter Seven, I demonstrated how I made the most of my trip to Bali, Indonesia, using my credit card rewards. Also, I've personally used other advanced strategies to travel the world without breaking the bank, and now I'm going to show you how you can do the same.

How to Maximize Your Credit Card Rewards

Maximizing credit card rewards is about more than just accumulating points or miles; it's about redeeming them at the right time (e.g., special promotions), for the right things. If travel is a priority for you, your objective should be to sync your credit card rewards with your lifestyle and financial goals.

By using these advanced travel hacking strategies, you can turn everyday purchases into luxury travel experiences, exclusive perks, and significant savings. Let's dive into how you can do this.

Strategically Redeem Your Rewards

How you redeem your rewards is just as important as how you earn them. For example, redeeming points for travel-related expenses like flights or hotel stays often provides better value than cash back.

> **Travel Rewards:** When you redeem points for travel-related expenses, your rewards can be worth more—sometimes up to 2-3 times the value of cash-back redemptions. This is one of the most valuable aspects of credit card rewards, and I recommend taking advantage of it if you're planning a vacation.

Pro Tip: If you're planning a vacation, consider using your points for flights or accommodations. This likely provides more value than redeeming them for cash back or gift cards.

Cashback vs. Points: If you're not planning a major trip soon, you might think that redeeming points for cash is the easiest way to go. However, ask yourself whether you could use those points for travel or other experiences. A little planning can stretch your rewards much further.

Take Advantage of Special Promotions

Credit card companies often run promotions or offer bonus categories that allow you to earn extra rewards. Timing your spending to match these promotions can boost your rewards balance significantly.

For example, some cards offer 5x points on specific categories like grocery purchases or gas station expenses for a limited time. The key is staying alert to these promotions to maximize them.

Quick Tip: Do you have a favorite shopping category, like groceries or dining out? Find out if any of your credit cards offer bonus rewards in these areas. Be sure to use them during promotional periods to rack up more rewards.

Chase Freedom cash-back calendar for 2025

Chase has just announced the bonus 5% cash-back categories for the first quarter of 2025. The categories for the rest of the year will be released soon.

- **January to March** (activate now): Grocery stores, fitness clubs and gym memberships and hair, nails and spa services, Norwegian Cruise Lines

The screenshot is an example of special promotion from Chase

Managing Annual Fees: Are They Worth It?

Some credit cards charge an annual fee, and while this might seem like an added cost, many of these cards offer valuable perks that make the fee worthwhile. But before committing, it's important to assess whether the rewards and benefits justify the cost.

When to Avoid Annual fees: If you're new to credit cards or just building your rewards portfolio, it's best to stick with cards that don't charge an annual fee. This allows you to earn rewards and build credit without paying extra.

When to Consider Annual Fees: Once you become more experienced with credit cards, you might find that some cards with annual fees offer substantial benefits such as travel insurance, airport lounge access, free upgrades, free meals, and even expedited security screening through programs like Global Entry and TSA PreCheck. These perks can significantly enhance your travel experience and convenience.

Personal Insight

When I first got the **Chase Sapphire Reserve®** card, the annual fee seemed steep. However, the perks quickly paid off—lounge access, travel insurance, and a huge welcome bonus. With my frequent travel schedule, it was a no-brainer. I later downgraded to the **Chase Sapphire Preferred®** to reduce the annual fee, which still allowed me to enjoy the benefits and rewards of the card. I also added the **Charles Schwab Amex Platinum Card**, aligning my travel rewards with my financial goals by transferring points into my brokerage account.

The *key takeaway* here is that high annual fee cards can provide exceptional value, but only if the benefits align with your lifestyle.

Double Your Rewards: Travel Hacking 101

Travel hacking is the practice of using credit card rewards and loyalty programs in tandem to get even more value from your spending. By combining your credit card rewards with airline and hotel loyalty programs, you can earn double (*sometimes triple*) rewards for a ***single*** transaction.

Double Down on Loyalty Programs: Many credit card companies partner with airlines and hotel chains. By linking your airline or hotel loyalty program to your credit card, you can earn points in both programs simultaneously. For example, booking a flight with your credit card rewards could also earn you frequent flier miles with the airline's loyalty program.

Upgrade Your Travel Experience: Use your credit card rewards to book economy class tickets, then use your loyalty points to upgrade to business or first class. This strategy often costs fewer points than booking directly in a premium class, saving you money while enhancing your travel experience.

Shop through Airline Portals: Many airlines offer shopping portals where you can earn bonus miles for purchases from everyday retailers. By using your credit card to make purchases through these portals, you double your rewards—earning both airline miles and credit card points.

The Value of Points

Maximizing the value of your credit card points is key to getting the most out of your spending. The value of points can vary depending on how you redeem them. Typically, travel-related redemptions offer more value than cash-back redemptions, and some cards offer bonus value when you use their travel portals.

For example, if you redeem points for travel-related expenses such as flights or hotel stays, you can often get more value than redeeming them for cash back. Here's how different cards offer value:

Chase Sapphire Preferred® gives you a 25% bonus when booking travel through the Chase Travel Portal. This means that 10,000 points could be worth $125 when redeemed for travel.

Chase Sapphire Reserve® offers 1.5 cents per point when booking travel through its portal, giving you a 50% boost in value.

American Express Membership Rewards® points can be worth around 1 cent when redeemed for flights through the American Express Travel portal, but when transferred to its airline partners, the value increases, especially when booking premium cabin flights.

Points' value can also fluctuate depending on your redemption options. For instance, using points for luxury travel perks or transferring them to airline or hotel partners can sometimes increase their value by 2x or more. This is why it's important to understand how to best use your points for maximum reward.

Transferring Points to Partners

One of the most powerful ways to maximize your rewards is by transferring points to airline or hotel partners. When you transfer points to these partners, you can often get significantly more value than if you redeem them through the credit card issuer's own portal. Here's how it works:

Chase Ultimate Rewards®: For example, when you transfer points from a Chase Sapphire Preferred® or Reserve® card to an airline like United Airlines or a hotel like Hyatt, your points can be worth 2x or more compared to redeeming them through Chase's Travel Portal. This can result in a higher-value redemption, especially for flights and hotel stays.

American Express Membership Rewards®: Transferring points from American Express to partners like Delta Airlines or Singapore Airlines can increase their value dramatically—up to 2 cents per point or more when booking premium cabin flights. This is especially beneficial for travelers seeking first-class or business-class experiences, where point values are generally higher.

Capital One Miles®: Transferring points to airline partners like JetBlue or Emirates can yield better redemption rates for flights, making this card a solid choice for frequent travelers.

Using transfer partners allows you to leverage your points for premium experiences, and often at a lower redemption cost than booking directly through a card's travel portal.

Point Value Breakdown

Below is a breakdown of points and miles values for several popular travel credit cards. This chart will help you understand how different cards reward you for your spending. Keep in mind that point values can fluctuate based on redemption options and changes by the issuer. Please refer to your card issuer for the most up-to-date information on point values.

Credit Card	Points for Travel	Points for Cash Back	Best Use
Chase Sapphire Preferred®	1.25 cents	1 cent	Travel
Chase Sapphire Reserve®	1.5 cents	1 cent	Premium Travel
American Express Platinum	1 cent	0.6 cents	Luxury travel & lounge access
American Express Gold	1 cent	0.6 cents	Dining, Travel
Capital One Venture Rewards	1 cent	1 cent	Travel (flights, hotels)
Capital One Venture X	1.5 cents	1 cent	Travel, Luxury perks
Regions Bank Prestige®	1.75 cents	1 cent	Dining, Entertainment, Travel
Citi Premier® Card	1 cent	0.5 cents	Travel, Dining
Citi Double Cash Card	1 cent	1 cent	Simple, non-categorized cash back
Chase Freedom Unlimited®	1 cent	1 cent	General purchases, 1.5% back on all spending
Discover it® Miles	1 cent	1 cent	Travel (redemption for travel purchases)

Ready to Take Action?

Congratulations! You now have the tools to strategically maximize your credit card rewards. By understanding how to earn, redeem, and transfer your points, you've unlocked the potential to turn everyday purchases into unforgettable experiences. Whether you're planning a dream vacation or seeking ways to save on everyday expenses, the key is to be intentional with your rewards strategy.

Start by evaluating your current credit cards and aligning them with your travel and financial goals. Remember to keep an eye on special promotions, make the most of bonus categories, and consider transferring your points to maximize their value. With the right approach, your credit cards can become powerful tools that help you achieve your goals—whether it's a luxurious getaway, a stronger financial future, or even both.

The most important step is applying these strategies to your daily spending now. The more consistent and strategic you are, the greater the rewards you'll reap.

Chapter 9 Questions

1. What is the difference between redeeming credit card points for travel and cash back? Why does travel often offer more value?

2. Which credit card(s) do you currently use the most? Are you maximizing the rewards potential of those cards?

3. How can you use the strategy of transferring points to increase the value of your rewards?

4. What are some strategies you can implement today to start maximizing your rewards (such as aligning cards with spending categories or tracking special promotions)?

5. After reviewing the Point Value Breakdown chart, which credit card would best align with your current spending habits and rewards goals?

Chapter 9 Maximizing Travel Rewards: Interactive Action Plan

Use this form to assess your current travel rewards strategy and identify actionable steps you can take to start maximizing your points. Think of this as your personal roadmap to becoming a travel hacker!

1. **Evaluate your current travel rewards strategy.**
    a. I actively track my points and make sure I'm using them for travel-related expenses (flights, hotels, car rentals).
    b. I primarily redeem points for cash back and need to focus more on travel redemptions.
    c. I use multiple credit cards for different categories but am unsure if I'm maximizing my points for travel.
    d. I don't track promotions or know when to redeem points for optimal value.

2. **Which travel goal are you focused on?** (Select one or more)
    a. Free flights to my favorite destinations
    b. Free hotel stays at luxury resorts or chains
    c. Travel upgrades (business/first-class, hotel upgrades)
    d. Using travel points to make family vacations more affordable
    e. Building a long-term travel rewards strategy for future trips

3. **Which strategy will you implement first to maximize travel rewards?** (Select one or more)

   a. Start transferring points to airline and hotel partners (e.g., from Chase Ultimate Rewards® to United or Hyatt) to maximize value.

   b. Redeem points for travel-related expenses instead of cash or gift cards to get higher value.

   c. Monitor special promotions or bonus categories (e.g., 5x points on certain purchases) to boost my rewards.

   d. Book travel during peak redemption periods (e.g., using points for flights when there are no blackout dates or taking advantage of transfer bonus offers).

4. **How are you planning to redeem your points?** (Select the option that applies to your next redemption)

   a. Redeem my points for a free flight and use transfer partners to get more value (e.g., transferring Chase points to United for an upgrade).

   b. Use points to cover hotel stays, especially with partners like Hyatt or Marriott, for additional benefits and discounts.

   c. Combine multiple points programs (e.g., Chase Ultimate Rewards® points for a flight and Amex Membership Rewards® points for a hotel stay).

   d. I'm planning to use my points for luxury travel upgrades (e.g., first-class using miles or booking premium cabin flights through transfer partners).

5. **Which credit card(s) do you currently use for travel rewards?** (Select all that apply)
   a. Chase Sapphire Preferred® or Reserve®
   b. American Express Platinum or Gold
   c. Capital One Venture Rewards or Venture X
   d. Citi Premier® or Citi Double Cash
   e. Regions Bank Prestige®
   f. Other (please specify): _____

6. **What will be your next step to maximize travel rewards?** (Select one)
   a. I will focus on using my points for premium travel redemptions, like flights and hotel stays.
   b. I will look into transferring points to airline or hotel partners for higher-value rewards.
   c. I will adjust my spending to match the best bonus categories for travel rewards.
   d. I will track my credit card's special promotions to take advantage of the best deals.

7. **Estimate how much you could save on your next vacation using these travel hacking strategies:**
   a. $0 - $500
   b. $500 - $1,000
   c. $1,000 - $2,000
   d. $2,000+
   e. Not sure yet, but I'm excited to start!

CHAPTER 10

ADVANCED CREDIT UTILIZATION STRATEGIES: WINNING THE CREDIT CARD GAME

Credit Cards are not free money. They are powerful tools for leverage when used strategically.

–Dr. Charley Thomas

Imagine this: a small adjustment in how you use your credit cards could unlock a higher credit score, lower interest rates, and better your financial opportunities. That's exactly what happened to one of my closest friends.

He was doing everything right—paying off his balances, earning cash-back rewards, and keeping his balances low. Yet, his credit score wasn't improving. Frustrated and confused, he came to me for advice, feeling like all his hard work was going unnoticed.

After we discussed how credit utilization works, a light bulb went off. He realized that while he was keeping low balances on individual cards, his overall credit utilization across all his cards was still too high, holding back his score.

With just a few adjustments—like lowering his overall utilization rate, timing his payments, and requesting a credit limit increase—he saw a dramatic boost in his score. These changes gave him better control over his credit and unlocked new financial doors. Today, he enjoys lower interest rates, better card offers, and even more confidence in managing his finances.

In this chapter, I'll show you how to do the same. These advanced strategies will help you leverage your credit cards to boost your credit score and open up exciting new financial opportunities.

Optimizing Credit Utilization: Why These Are Advanced Strategies

These strategies go beyond the basics of simply paying off your credit card balances and avoiding late fees. They involve understanding the nuanced factors that credit bureaus and lenders consider when evaluating your credit profile. Here's why they're considered advanced:

1. **Leveraging Utilization Percentages**
    Most people don't realize how their overall credit utilization—across all cards—affects their score more than individual card balances. Managing this effectively requires a bird's-eye view of your finances.

2. **Timing Payments Strategically**
    Instead of just paying by the due date, you learn to make payments before your statement date to reduce reported

balances. This advanced technique ensures your credit report reflects the lowest possible utilization.

3. **Requesting Limit Increases Proactively**
   Asking for credit limit increases at the right time, while maintaining good financial habits, helps lower your utilization without requiring lifestyle changes.

These strategies require attention to detail and proactive planning, but they yield results that basic credit management practices cannot achieve. By mastering these techniques, you position yourself for better interest rates, credit offers, and long-term financial success.

Strategy 1: Managing Overall Credit Utilization

One of the most important steps in improving your credit score is managing your overall credit utilization. While it's common to focus on the utilization of individual cards, the **overall utilization across all your credit cards** is what truly matters most. However, **if you only have one credit card**, managing your utilization becomes even more crucial, as the balance on that single card directly affects your score.

How to Calculate Overall Credit Utilization

To calculate your overall credit utilization, add up the credit limits and balances of all your credit cards. Here's how it works if you have multiple cards:

> **Example:**
> Card 1: Credit Limit = $5,000, Balance = $1,000

Card 2: Credit Limit = $10,000, Balance = $2,000

Card 3: Credit Limit = $15,000, Balance = $3,000

Total Credit Limit = $30,000

Total Balance = $6,000

Overall Utilization Rate = Total Balance ÷ Total Credit Limit × 100

Overall Utilization Rate = $6,000 ÷ $30,000 × 100 = **20%**

For those with only one credit card, the overall utilization rate is simply calculated as the balance on that card divided by its limit.

Example for One Card:

Card 1: Credit Limit = $5,000, Balance = $1,000

Overall Utilization Rate = $1,000 ÷ $5,000 × 100 = **20%**

Even with a single card, **keeping your utilization below 30%** is important. But to maximize your credit score, it's ideal to aim for **under 10%**. A lower utilization rate demonstrates to lenders that you're using your credit responsibly, which can help improve your credit score over time.

Recommendation: Keep your overall credit utilization rate below 10% to see maximum improvements in your credit score, even if you have only one card.

Charge Cards and Their Role in Credit Utilization

Many people think all credit cards affect their credit utilization rate, but **charge cards** (like the American Express Platinum) are a different breed. Unlike traditional credit cards, charge cards don't have a pre-set credit limit, meaning **they don't impact your credit utilization** ratio. This can seem like an advantage for those trying to keep their utilization low.

However, even though **charge cards** don't factor into credit utilization, the **amount you spend** still shows up on your **credit report**. This means if you're spending large amounts, it could still influence how lenders view your overall financial health and might affect your **debt-to-income ratio**, which is another factor that lenders consider.

The Risk of Late Payments on Charge Cards

One crucial point to remember with charge cards is that **late payments** carry a **serious penalty**. Unlike credit cards, which allow you to carry a balance and avoid interest (if paid within the grace period), **American Express** and other issuers can remove your **grace period entirely** if you make a late payment. This means interest will be charged **from the date of purchase**, not the payment due date. This can quickly turn into unexpected financial charges, so it's vital to stay on top of your payments.

Strategy 2: Timing Your Payments to Lower Utilization

Managing the timing of your payments is one of the most effective ways to keep your credit utilization low when issuers report your balances to the credit bureaus. Here's how you can use timing to your advantage:

Pay-As-You-Go Strategy: Use Your Credit Card Like a Debit Card

An effective strategy is to treat your credit card like a debit card—spend only what you've budgeted, and pay off the balance immediately or as you go. This prevents the accumulation of large balances that could hurt your utilization rate.

Instead of waiting until your statement due date, make payments right after a purchase. This will keep your utilization low throughout the month and ensure your credit score stays in good standing.

Timing Payments Before the Statement Date

Even if you don't make immediate payments, you can still time your payments around your billing cycle. For example, if your billing cycle ends on the 25th of the month, make a payment before that date to lower the balance that will get reported to the credit bureaus. This lowers your reported utilization and boosts your score.

> **Recommendation:** Schedule payments throughout the month, especially after big purchases, to keep your utilization low before issuers report to the bureaus. Stay ahead of your spending to maintain a healthy credit score.

Strategy 3: Requesting Credit Limit Increases

One powerful way to manage your credit utilization and improve your credit score is by **requesting a credit limit increase**. Many credit card issuers will allow you to increase your limit every 6 months, especially if you've been a responsible cardholder by making on-time payments and keeping your balances low. This simple strategy can help improve your overall credit utilization rate, which can have a positive impact on your credit score.

Why a Credit Limit Increase Helps

A higher credit limit means you have more available credit, which lowers your credit utilization ratio—especially if you don't increase your spending. For example, if you have a $1,000 balance on a card with a $5,000 limit, your utilization is 20%. If your credit limit is increased to $7,500 and you maintain the same $1,000 balance, your utilization drops to **13.3%**, which can boost your credit score.

Soft Pulls for Credit Limit Increases

One of the best things about requesting a credit limit increase is that certain banks, including **Chase**, **Capital One**, and **Discover**, perform a **soft pull** on your credit report. A soft pull doesn't impact your credit score, making it a low-risk option for increasing your credit limit. Always check with your issuer to confirm their specific process before making the request.

Keeping Your Income Current

It's also important to keep your **income current** on file with your card issuers. Many credit card companies use your reported income to assess your creditworthiness when deciding whether to approve a credit limit increase. If you've had a change in income—whether an increase from a raise or new job—updating this information could help you secure a higher limit. Keep in mind, though, that banks will usually only approve increases that align with your income and overall credit profile.

Strategy 4: Credit Limit Transfers

Reallocating credit limits between cards under the same issuer is a powerful way to fund large purchases, lower your utilization ratio, and improve your credit score.

What It Is:

Reallocating credit limits means transferring available credit from one card to another within the same issuer's portfolio.

Why It Matters:

Credit utilization—the ratio of your credit card balances to your credit limits—is a significant factor in determining your credit score. By lowering your utilization, you can improve your credit score and access better financing options.

Benefits:

1. **Maximize Strategic Spending**

   Increase the limit on a 0% APR card to fund large purchases or investments.

2. **Lower Utilization**

   Reducing your utilization ratio can boost your credit score, positioning you for better interest rates on loans or other credit products.

Steps to Execute:

1. **Identify Eligible Cards**

   Review your accounts to find cards from the same issuer (e.g., Chase, American Express).

2. **Assess Your Needs**

   Determine which card requires a higher limit (e.g., a 0% APR card for investments).

3. **Request the Transfer**

   Call customer service and request a credit limit reallocation.

4. **Use Responsibly**

   Always have a repayment plan to avoid over-leveraging your finances.

Example:

If you transfer $5,000 from a rewards card to a 0% APR card, you can fund a $10,000 renovation interest-free while simultaneously lowering your utilization ratio.

Advanced Tip: Ensure the card receiving the higher limit maintains a utilization rate below 30% for maximum impact on your credit score.

Strategy 5: Understanding and Using Grace Periods

A grace period is the interest-free time between your statement date and your payment due date. This allows you to avoid interest charges if you pay your balance in full. Here's how popular issuers define their grace periods and tips to maximize their benefits:

Grace Period Chart with Key Tips

Issuer	Grace Period	Key Tip
American Express	At least 25 days	Pay in full by the due date to maintain an interest-free period.
Capital One	Minimum 25 days	Use your billing cycle end date to time payments and stay interest-free.
Chase	Minimum 21 days	Avoid late payments to ensure you retain your grace period privileges.
Citi	Up to 23 days	Make full payments early to prevent potential interest charges.
Discover	Minimum 23 days	Monitor your cycle to avoid balances that could impact grace periods.
Regions	21 days	Track billing cycles and aim for full payments to benefit from grace.
Truist, USAA, Navy Federal	Typically 25 days	Keep balances low and ensure on-time payments to maximize grace periods.

Note: Grace periods vary by card. Review your cardholder agreement to make the most of this valuable feature.

Now that you have these advanced strategies, you're in an exceptional position to unlock greater financial opportunities. These approaches go beyond simply paying off your balances—they require a strategic mindset and a proactive commitment to managing your credit. While they demand effort and attention to detail, the rewards are worth it because they put you in control of your financial destiny.

By focusing on reducing your overall utilization, timing your payments effectively, and requesting credit limit increases, you're not just improving your credit score—you're building a foundation for long-term wealth and financial independence. Each small change you make today creates opportunities for tomorrow.

Take inspiration from my friend who used these same strategies to improve his credit. With just a few deliberate adjustments, he unlocked better financial opportunities, gained confidence, and moved closer to achieving his goals. You too can use these steps to turn small changes into meaningful progress. Whether it's lowering your utilization rate, perfectly timing your payments, or requesting a credit limit increase, each action you take brings you closer to financial freedom.

With consistent effort and determination, your credit cards can go from being a financial hurdle to a powerful tool for building the life you've always envisioned. Success isn't about perfection— it's about making thoughtful choices and leveraging the resources at your disposal. Your journey to financial empowerment begins now, with the decisions you make today.

So take that first step. Use the Credit Utilization Tracker and Action Plan tools to put these strategies into action. Each step you take moves you closer to achieving your goals. Remember, the power is in your hands. Let your credit cards work for you, not against you, and embrace the opportunities that lie ahead.

Chapter 10 Questions

1. How can optimizing your credit utilization directly impact your ability to secure better financial opportunities?

2. What is your current credit limit utilization rate, and what steps can you take to reduce it to under 10%?

3. Have you thought about requesting a credit limit increase or reallocating your credit limits? How would these actions affect your utilization and credit score?

4. Have you considered timing your credit card payments differently to improve your credit score? How might this change your strategy?

5. How can reallocating credit limits between cards help you fund large purchases or lower your utilization?

Chapter 10 Tools and resources:

Take a moment to complete the Credit Utilization Tracker and Action Plan. These small steps will set you on the path to strengthening your credit strategy and achieving your financial goals.

Step 1: Credit Utilization Tracker

Use this tracker to monitor your credit card balances and ensure your credit utilization stays within your target range. Update it monthly to track progress.

Credit Card Name	Credit Limit ($)	Current Balance ($)	Utilization Rate (%)	Target Utilization Rate (%)	Transferred Limit ($)
Card 1					
Card 2					
Card 3					
Totals					

How to Use:

1. List all your credit cards in the first column.
2. Enter the credit limit for each card in the second column.
3. Enter the current balance in the third column.
4. Calculate your utilization rate for each card: *(Current Balance ÷ Credit Limit) × 100*.
5. Set a target utilization rate (e.g., 10% or below).

Step 2: Credit Utilization Action Plan

Follow this step-by-step guide to optimize your credit utilization and improve your credit score.

2.1: Assess Your Current Utilization

1. List all your credit cards and calculate your overall utilization rate (total balances ÷ total credit limits × 100).
2. Identify which cards have high utilization rates.

2.2: Set Your Goals

1. Short-term Goal: Lower overall utilization to below 30%.
2. Long-term Goal: Aim for utilization under 10% for maximum credit score improvement.

2.3: Implement Strategies

1. **Request a Credit Limit Increase:**
   a. Contact your issuer to increase your limit.
   b. Focus on cards with low balances but high credit limits to maximize the impact.
2. **Reallocate Credit Limits:**
   a. Identify cards with unused limits that can be shifted to a 0% APR or high-spending card.
   b. Contact the issuer to request a credit limit transfer.

3. **Pay As You Go:**
   a. Treat your credit card like a debit card. Pay off balances immediately after making purchases.

4. **Time Your Payments:**
   a. Make payments before the statement date to lower the balance reported to credit bureaus.

5. **Avoid High Balances:**
   a. Use multiple cards for expenses to distribute balances evenly and keep individual card utilization low.

Step 3: Monitor Progress

1. Use the Credit Utilization Tracker to update balances and utilization rates monthly.
2. Adjust your spending and payments based on progress.

Step 4: Reflect and Adjust

1. Reflect on what strategies worked best.
2. Plan for future goals, such as securing better interest rates or rewards cards.

CHAPTER 11

ADVANCED CREDIT
CARD STRATEGIES

---

*When used wisely, credit cards are not liabilities but
tools to unlock wealth and opportunity.*

—Dr. Charley Thomas

For many people, credit cards feel like a double-edged sword—
useful for convenience but often tied to debt and financial stress. It's
easy to see them as a burden rather than a tool. But what if you could
flip the script and use your credit cards to build wealth and achieve
big goals?

That's exactly what one of my clients learned. During one of
our conversations, he said, "I use my credit cards for everything to
get cash back, but I'm not sure what else I should be doing." That
simple statement opened the door to an entirely new perspective.

He was already making smart choices, like earning rewards and
paying off balances, but he hadn't tapped into advanced strategies
that could take his financial game to the next level. Together, we

created a step-by-step plan to align his credit card use with a long-time dream: purchasing a multifamily property where he could live in one unit and rent out the others.

We focused on three key strategies:

1. **Maximizing rewards** to build additional savings and free up cash flow.
2. **Strategically managing credit utilization** to improve his credit score and qualify for better financing options.
3. **Leveraging 0% APR offers** to fund property-related costs without incurring high-interest charges.

Within months, he wasn't just using credit cards for everyday purchases—he was using them as a tool to build wealth. By applying these strategies, he turned what once seemed like a distant goal into a tangible achievement. The property didn't just provide a home; it became a source of passive income and opened doors to future opportunities.

In this chapter, I'll share the same strategies so you can turn your financial dreams into reality. Whether you're looking to invest, build wealth, or maximize your credit card benefits, these advanced techniques will give you the tools to win the credit card game.

Through these advanced strategies, you too can take control of your finances and turn everyday spending into a wealth-building powerhouse.

Reward Optimization Strategies

The first step to maximizing your credit card's potential is to optimize the rewards you earn. Let's start with leveraging sign-up bonuses

Strategy 1: Leverage Sign-Up Bonuses

Sign-up bonuses are one of the fastest ways to earn significant rewards. Many credit cards offer bonuses worth $500–$1,000 when you meet minimum spending requirements, typically within the first three months.

How to Maximize Sign-Up Bonuses

1. **Plan Large Purchases:** Align big expenses, like home upgrades, business equipment, or travel, with new card sign-ups to meet spending thresholds without overspending.
2. **Combine Bonuses and Rewards:** Use sign-up bonuses alongside ongoing cash-back or point-earning strategies for a multiplier effect.
3. **Redeem Strategically:** Invest bonuses in a brokerage account, use them to pay down debt, or allocate them toward a long-term financial goal.

Home Office Upgrade: A $500 Reward Win

When Trina, a freelance graphic designer, planned to upgrade her home office, she saw it as an opportunity to maximize her credit card benefits. She applied for a rewards credit card offering a $500 bonus for spending $3,000 in three months. By using the card to purchase her new desk, chair, software and monitor, she easily met the spending requirement. Trina paid off the balance immediately and invested her $500 bonus

---

> into ETF VOO. Over the next two years, that bonus earned her an additional \$112 —a small but powerful step toward building wealth.
>
> Now that you've seen how others have successfully leveraged these strategies, it's your turn to build a wealth-building plan tailored to your goals using these same strategies.

Action Plan: Get the Most Out of Your Next Sign-Up Bonus

1. **Identify Your Expense**
   - What's the next big purchase you're planning? (e.g., home office upgrade, travel, or education): _____
   - Estimated cost: \$_____

2. **Research Credit Card Options**
   - Use a comparison tool or visit websites to find a credit card that matches your expense.
   - Card name: _____
   - Sign-up bonus amount: \$_____
   - Spending requirement (within X months): \$_____

3. **Create a Spending Timeline**
   - How will you meet the requirement? Break it down by months or categories.
     - Month 1 Spend: \$_____
     - Month 2 Spend: \$_____

4. **Plan for Your Bonus**
   - Decide how to use the bonus for your financial goals (circle one):
     - Save (e.g., high-yield account, emergency fund).

- Invest (e.g., brokerage account, index fund).
- Pay Down Debt.

Maximizing rewards through sign-up bonuses can provide the extra cash-back savings needed to jumpstart your investments or build a real estate down payment fund, as explained in the next strategies.

Strategy 2: Turn Your Cash-back into Investments

Redirecting your cash-back rewards into investment accounts unlocks their full potential.

How It Works

1. Use credit cards offering 1%-5% cash back on everyday purchases.
2. Transfer rewards into a brokerage or retirement account.
3. Automate monthly contributions to an index fund or high-yield savings account.

Impact Over Time

Small rewards can add up to big savings. For instance, investing $100 in rewards monthly could grow to:

- $1,200 in 1 year.
- Over $7,000 in 5 years.
- Nearly $18,500 in 10 years.

Thanks to compound interest, your earnings will generate additional growth over time.

How this works: Using a credit card that gives 2% cash back on your everyday spending can quickly add up. For example, spending $2,000 in a month earns $40 in cash back. If you also take advantage of higher reward rates on specific categories, you could easily save $100 a month to put toward your financial goals.

Turning Points into Profits

One year, I used my American Express Membership Rewards points to deposit $1,100 into my brokerage account through the Charles Schwab Amex Platinum card. These points, which would have been worth far less as a simple cash-out, became a meaningful addition to my portfolio.

Advanced Tip: Combine rewards from multiple cards into a single investment account for faster growth.

Action Plan: Start Investing Your Rewards

1. **Calculate Monthly Cash-Back Potential**
   o Monthly spending estimate: $_____
   o Cash-back rate (e.g., 2%): _____%
   o Estimated rewards per month: $_____

2. **Choose an Investment Vehicle**
   (Circle one)
   o Brokerage account
   o High-yield savings account
   o Retirement fund (e.g., IRA)
   o Other: _____

3. **Automate Your Investment**
   o Set up a monthly transfer of cash-back rewards to your investment account.
   o Amount to Invest Monthly: $_____
4. **Track Growth**
   o Use an app or spreadsheet to monitor your investments over time.
   o Target Annual Growth: _____%

Once your cash-back rewards are generating returns, they can help fund goals like property investments or business expansion, as discussed in the following strategies.

Investment and Wealth-Building Strategies

Strategy 3: Leverage Credit for Real Estate

Credit cards can play a surprising role in real estate, from building a down payment fund to financing renovations.

Strategies for Real Estate:

1. **Grow a Down Payment Fund**
    a. Deposit cash-back rewards into a high-yield savings account or CD.
    b. Combine these rewards with sign-up bonuses to accelerate your savings.

Example: If you deposit $1,200 annually into a 4% interest savings account, your balance grows to $2,472 in two years. Add a $500 sign-up bonus, and you're well on your way to a down payment.

---

2. **Finance Renovations with 0% APR**
    Use a 0% APR credit card for property improvements and repay during the promotional period.Increase property value without incurring interest.

3. **0% APR for fees before closing cost**
    Use a 0% APR card to cover pre-closing fees, like appraisals or inspections, to manage upfront costs without incurring interest.

Duplex Renovation: From 10k to 20k

Dwayne, a first-time property investor, used a $10,000 credit card with a 0% APR to renovate a duplex. He prioritized high-

---

impact upgrades, including repainting for $2,500, installing new flooring for $3,000, and replacing outdated kitchen appliances for $4,500. Within six months, these improvements increased the property's value by $20,000. With both units rented at $1,200 each. Dwayne's $10,000 renovation not only increased the property value by $20,000 but also brought in an additional $500 in monthly rental income. He will pay off the initial investment within two years.

Credit cards aren't just for small purchases—they can be tools for major milestones like buying and renovating property. By using rewards and 0% APR offers wisely, you can unlock real estate opportunities that once felt out of reach.

Action Plan: Turn Credit into Real Estate Wealth

1. **Set Your Real Estate Goals**
   o Target property (type or location): _____
   o Down payment goal: $_____

2. **Grow a Down Payment Fund**
   o Annual cash-back/Bonus target: $_____
   o Savings account type (circle one): High-yield | CD | Other
   o Annual interest rate: _____%

3. **Plan for Renovations**
   o Estimated renovation budget: $_____
   o 0% APR Card name: _____
   o Promotional period: _____ months

4. **Repayment Strategy**
   o Monthly payment goal: $_____

o   Completion date: _____

Strategy 4: Treat Your Finances Like a Business

Think of your personal finances as a business. Every dollar counts, and every expense or reward should serve a purpose.

Earn More: Use rewards cards or try a side hustle to boost income.

Spend Smarter: Use credit cards that offer the best rewards for your spending habits.

Invest Strategically: Redirect rewards to grow your savings or investment accounts.

Manage Debt Wisely: Take advantage of 0% APR offers to fund growth without paying high-interest rates.

**Side Hustle Success: Growing a business
with 0% APR**

When I started managing my finances like a business, I used a 0% APR card to purchase inventory for a side hustle. The profits generated during the promotional period not only covered the card balance but also added to my savings. By keeping detailed records of every dollar earned and spent, I saw my financial goals as milestones on a roadmap to success.

Interactive Plan:

Write down three ways you can treat your finances like a business:

1.

2.

3.

Example: Track all rewards and bonuses in a spreadsheet to ensure maximum utilization.

Adopting a business mindset makes transitioning to business credit seamless, opening up opportunities for higher credit limits and targeted rewards.

Generational and Business Growth Strategies

Strategy 5: Leveraging Business Credit for Growth

If you have a side hustle or business, integrating business credit can help you scale faster.

Why Leverage Business Credit?

1. **Access to Higher Limits**

   Business credit cards often offer higher credit limits than personal cards, enabling you to fund larger projects or purchases.

2. **Separate Finances**

   Keeping personal and business expenses separate simplifies bookkeeping and protects your personal credit from business-related debt.

3. **Maximize Tax Deductions**

   Many business expenses charged to a business credit card—such as travel, supplies, and marketing are tax-deductible.

4. **Unlock Perks and Benefits**

   Business credit cards often offer perks tailored to entrepreneurs, such as higher cash-back rewards on office supplies, free employee cards, and travel credits.

5. **Build a Business Credit Profile**

   Establishing strong business credit can lead to future opportunities like business loans, leases, and lines of credit.

How to Leverage Business Credit Strategically

1. **Identify Your Business Needs**

   a. **Inventory or supplies:** Use business credit to manage cash flow during purchasing cycles.

    b. **Marketing:** Fund advertising campaigns or product launches with a 0% APR card.

    c. **Expansion:** Finance equipment, technology, or other investments to grow your operations.

2. **Choose the Right Business Credit Card**

    a. Look for cards with rewards categories that match your spending habits (e.g., cash back on office supplies, bonus points on advertising).

    b. Consider 0% APR introductory offers to finance upfront costs interest-free.

3. **Use Rewards to Reinvest in Your Business**

    a. Redeem cash-back rewards to offset business expenses or build a reserve fund.

    b. Transfer points to travel programs for business trips, saving on flights or hotels.

4. **Separate Personal and Business Finances**

    Open a business checking account and use your business credit card exclusively for business-related purchases.

5. **Track and Optimize Spending**

    Use bookkeeping software or apps (e.g., QuickBooks, Wave) to categorize and monitor business expenses.

From Passion to Profits

When I turned my passion for wellness into a tea business, I used a business credit card with a 0% APR offer to finance my first bulk inventory order. By spreading the payments over 12 months, I preserved my cash flow while building my product line. The card's rewards program also helped reduce costs—

cash-back rewards were reinvested into marketing campaigns, leading to higher sales.

This strategy allowed me to scale the business quickly without risking my personal finances.

Interactive Plan: Business Credit Growth Strategy

Step 1: Assess Your Business Needs

What do you need to fund (e.g., inventory, marketing, travel)?

Example: $5,000 for a product launch.

Step 2: Choose a Business Credit Card

Research cards that align with your goals:

0% APR duration: _____ months

Cash-back or points rewards: _____

Perks (e.g., travel credits, employee cards): _____

Step 3: Create a Spending and Repayment Plan

Planned monthly spending: $_____

Monthly repayment goal (for 0% APR balances): $_____

Target monthly rewards earned: $_____

Step 4: Reinforce Your Business Credit Profile

Pay balances on time and in full whenever possible.

Monitor your business credit score through Dun & Bradstreet, Experian, or Equifax Business.

Step 5: Reinvest Rewards

List how you'll reinvest rewards into your business:

Example: Use $500 in cash-back rewards for marketing ads on social media.

Advanced Tip: Converting a Side Hustle into a Business

If you're ready to formalize your side hustle into a business, here's how to do it:

1. **Register Your Business**
   a. Choose a legal structure (LLC, sole proprietorship, etc.) and file with your state.
   b. Obtain an Employer Identification Number (EIN) from the IRS if needed.
2. **Open a Business Bank Account**
   Keep business funds separate for better tracking and easier tax filing.
3. **Apply for a Business Credit Card**
   Use your personal credit as a guarantor if your business credit profile is still new.
4. **Set Goals**
   Define measurable business objectives to fund with your credit card.

Once you've established a strong financial foundation for yourself, it's time to think about the next generation. Teaching your child about credit can set them up for a lifetime of success.

Strategy 6: Build Generational Wealth through Credit

Teaching your child responsible credit card use is more than just a life lesson—it's a powerful move in the credit card game to set them up for a lifetime of financial opportunities. It fosters trust and equips them with confidence, knowing they have a financial foundation to support their goals. It also instills a sense of responsibility and financial independence, giving them the tools to make informed decisions throughout their lives. By leveraging advanced techniques like adding your child as an authorized user, you can strategically lay the groundwork for their creditworthiness while embedding financial literacy into their daily life.

Setting Up Your Child as an Authorized User

1. **Use Your Credit as a Launchpad for Theirs**

   When you add your child as an authorized user on a credit card with a strong history, they inherit the benefits of your responsible credit behavior. This gives them a head start in building a solid credit score before they ever open their first credit account.

   Key Benefit: A strong credit profile at 18 unlocks lower interest rates, better loan terms, and access to premium credit cards that might otherwise take years to qualify for.

2. **Choose the Right Credit Card Strategically**
   Select a card with:

   a. Low utilization (ideally under 30% of the credit limit).

   b. A long, consistent history of on-time payments.

   c. Rewards categories that align with shared expenses (e.g., groceries, gas), teaching them how to earn rewards responsibly.

3. **Set Clear Parameters for Use**

   Use spending limits or monitor transactions to teach budgeting skills. For example, allocate $50 per month for specific expenses like school supplies, fuel, or personal items. Tie spending privileges to lessons on credit, such as explaining how interest works or how rewards are earned.

Additional Note on Long-Term Benefits:

Parents who use this strategy not only help their child build a strong financial foundation but also foster confidence in managing credit responsibly. For example, adding a child as an authorized user on a card with a consistent payment history can elevate their credit score, enabling them to secure better loans and lower interest rates early in adulthood.

A Wealth-Building Approach: Practical Applications
Credit Score Building

Adding your child as an authorized user on a credit card you've had for years can give them a strong start with their credit score— potentially reaching the 700s by the time they turn 18. A high credit score can help them qualify for better loans and save thousands of interest over their lifetime.

Reward Integration

Use their authorized purchases to accumulate rewards for shared goals, such as saving for college expenses or family travel. For example, the points earned from their spending could help reduce out-of-pocket costs for future needs.

Future Financial Leverage:

A high credit score positions your child to qualify for better financial products early in adulthood, such as student loans with favorable terms, car loans with low interest rates, or even their own premium credit cards.

A Head Start to Financial Success

When my clients added their 16-year-old as an authorized user, they chose a card with a 10 year history and low utilization. They used the opportunity to teach budgeting and rewards optimization. By the time their child turned 18, they had a credit score of 745 and had saved $1,200 in cash-back rewards to use for college expenses. The process not only built their child's credit but also ingrained a lifelong habit of financial responsibility.

> **Key Takeaway:** Adding your child as an authorized user is an advanced credit strategy that builds generational wealth and financial literacy.

A strong start with credit gives them leverage to secure better financial products and achieve long-term goals.

Teaching them how to use credit cards responsibly ensures they approach credit as a tool for growth, not a liability.

Action Plan: Set Up Your Child for Credit Success

1. **Choose a Card**
   - o   Card name: _____
   - o   Credit limit: $_____
   - o   Payment history (circle one): Excellent | Good | Fair

2. **Set Spending Rules**
   - o   Monthly spending limit for child: $_____
   - o   Allowed purchases (e.g., school supplies, gas): _____

3. **Teach Credit Basics**
   o Schedule a family meeting to explain:
     ▪ What credit scores mean.
     ▪ How to pay balances in full each month.
     ▪ Why utilization should stay below 30%.

4. **Monitor Progress Together**
   o Credit tracker app/Tool: _____
   o Monthly credit score check date: _____

This strategy enables you to play the credit card game at the next level—by equipping the next generation with the tools to win.

In this chapter, you've learned how to use credit cards as powerful tools to achieve your financial goals.

1. **Maximize Rewards**: Capture high-value sign-up bonuses and redirect cash-back rewards into investments for long-term growth, just like Trina did with her $500 bonus.
2. **Invest Strategically**: Turn everyday spending into a source of compounding wealth by depositing rewards into savings or brokerage accounts.
3. **Leverage Credit for Real Estate**: Use cash-back savings and 0% APR offers to fund property purchases or renovations, as Dwayne did to increase his duplex's value by $20,000.
4. **Treat Finances Like a Business**: Approach your personal finances with the mindset of a CEO—track expenses, optimize rewards, and invest wisely to fuel growth.
5. **Scale with Business Credit**: Utilize business credit to fund your ventures, separate expenses, and reinvest rewards into opportunities for expansion.

6. **Build Generational Wealth**: Equip the next generation with financial literacy and a strong credit profile by adding them as authorized users on your credit card.

These six strategies show how credit cards can go beyond everyday conveniences to become tools for building wealth and opportunity. Whether you're starting small, like Trina, or taking bold steps like Dwayne, the credit card game is yours to win.

Choose one strategy, commit to it, and watch your financial goals take shape. Play the credit card game with purpose—and set yourself up for a lifetime of wins.

Chapter 11 Questions:

1. Which strategy feels most relevant to your current financial situation? Why?

2. What upcoming expense could you align with a credit card sign-up bonus?

3. What are three ways you can redirect cash-back rewards to grow your savings or investments?

4. How can you integrate credit into your plans for real estate or business growth?

5. If you were to teach someone about credit, what would be the first lesson you'd share?

CHAPTER 12

THE CREDIT CARD GAME ASSESSMENT

Now that you've completed this book, it's time to turn your knowledge into action. This final chapter is designed to help you assess where you stand in the credit card game, identify your strengths and weaknesses, and create a clear path toward turning your credit cards into financial assets.

Step 1: Assess Your Current Credit Card Situation

Take a moment to reflect on your credit card usage. Use the questions below to evaluate your current standing:

1. How many credit cards do you currently have? Are they helping or hurting your financial goals?
2. Do you know your current credit score? What factors are influencing it?
3. What is your total credit card debt? Is it manageable, or are you struggling with high balances?

4. Are you paying your balances in full each month, or are you carrying a balance?

5. Are you earning rewards with your **cards or simply accumulating debt?**

Step 2: Define Your Financial Goals

As discussed in Chapter Five, setting financial goals is crucial to winning the credit card game. Take a moment to outline your goals:

1. **Short-Term Goals** (3-6 months):
   Example: Pay off $2,000 in credit card debt.
2. **Long-Term Goals** (1-3 years):
   Example: Build a credit score of 750+ and accumulate $500 in rewards points for a vacation.

Step 3: Create Your Credit Card Strategy

Use the following steps to develop a winning strategy tailored to your situation:

1. **Evaluate Your Current Cards:**
   Are the cards you currently hold the best ones for your financial goals? Should you close some accounts or apply for new cards with better benefits?
2. **Choose the Right Credit Cards:**
   Based on Chapter Six, are you using the right credit cards for your spending habits and rewards preferences? Make a plan to apply for cards that align with your goals.

3. **Plan Your Debt Management:**

   As outlined in Chapter Eight, create a strategy to manage or pay off any existing credit card debt, focusing on high-interest cards first.

4. **Maximize Your Rewards:**

   Consider your daily spending habits and adjust them to maximize rewards (Chapter Seven). Are you making the most of cashback, travel rewards, or points?

Step 4: Monitor and Adjust

To ensure you're continually winning the credit card game, commit to regular check-ins:

1. **Monthly Review**

   Check your credit card balances, payment history, and rewards earned. Adjust spending or payment strategies if needed.

2. **Quarterly Review**

   Assess your progress toward your financial goals. Have your short-term goals been met? Are you on track with your long-term goals?

Step 5: Stay Committed to the Game

Winning the credit card game requires discipline, focus, and continuous learning. Remember the rules and strategies you've learned in this book, and stay committed to using credit cards as tools to build wealth, not liabilities.

1. **Keep Learning**: Stay updated on credit card news, such as new offers, reward programs, and changes to terms.
2. **Be Flexible**: Financial goals can change over time. Be willing to adjust your credit card strategy to adapt to new opportunities or challenges.

You Are Now in Control

The credit card game is about understanding how to turn a potential liability into an asset. With the right mindset, knowledge, and strategy, you can make your credit cards work for you, building credit, earning rewards, and achieving financial freedom.

Remember, the game isn't about perfection—it's about progress. Use this assessment as a guide to continue playing smart, adjusting your strategy as needed, and ultimately turning credit into an asset that enhances your financial life.

Example 1
Step 1: Assess Your Current Credit Card Situation

Sarah's Current Situation

Sarah has three credit cards with the following details:

Card 1:

Type: Cashback Card
Credit Limit: $5,000
Current Balance: $2,000
Interest Rate: 18% APR
Rewards: 1% cashback on all purchases

Card 2:

Type: Travel Rewards Card
Credit Limit: $7,500
Current Balance: $4,500
Interest Rate: 20% APR
Rewards: 2x miles on travel purchases, 1x miles on all other purchases

Card 3:

Type: Retail Store Card
Credit Limit: $2,000
Current Balance: $0
Interest Rate: 25% APR

Rewards: 5% discount on store purchases

Sarah's Evaluation:

Sarah is carrying a balance on two of her three cards, with the highest balance on her travel rewards card. She's unsure whether she's maximizing her rewards and concerned about the high-interest rates on the balances. Her current credit score is 690, which she knows could be better.

Step 2: Define Your Financial Goals

Sarah's Financial Goals

After reviewing her situation, Sarah sets both short-term and long-term financial goals.

1. **Short-Term Goal (next 6 months)**
   a. Pay off the $2,000 balance on her cashback card.
   b. Improve her credit score to 720 by lowering her credit utilization.
2. **Long-Term Goal (next 2 years)**
   a. Earn 100,000 travel miles for a dream vacation while avoiding carrying balances on her cards.
   b. Build her credit score to 750+ by consistently paying off her balances.

Step 3: Create Your Credit Card Strategy

Now, Sarah needs to build a strategy to achieve her goals.

1. **Evaluate Current Cards**

   Card 1 (Cashback Card)

   Sarah is carrying a balance with an 18% APR. Since this is her lowest interest rate card, she decides to pay off the balance first while making minimum payments on the others.

   Card 2 (Travel Rewards Card)

   While she's earning miles on this card, the 20% APR is costing her. Sarah resolves to stop making purchases on this card until the balance is significantly reduced or paid off. Once her balance is manageable, she will resume using this card to accumulate miles for her long-term goal.

   Card 3 (Retail Card)

   Sarah rarely shops at this store, and the 25% APR is too high. She decides to keep the card open (to help her credit utilization), but she won't use it unless absolutely necessary.

2. **Choose the Right Credit Cards**

   Focus on Card 1:

   Sarah will prioritize paying off the balance on her cashback card, which will help her avoid further interest charges and improve her credit utilization ratio.

Rewards Strategy:

After paying down her debt, Sarah plans to primarily use her travel rewards card (Card 2) for purchases in categories that earn double miles. She will make sure to pay off the balance in full each month to avoid high-interest charges.

3. **Plan Debt Management**

Debt Payoff Strategy:

Using the snowball method, Sarah will first focus on paying off the $2,000 balance on her cashback card, followed by her travel rewards card. She commits to making an extra payment of $250 per month on Card 1. Once that card is paid off, she'll apply the same strategy to Card 2.

4. **Maximize Rewards**

Short-Term:

For now, Sarah will stop using her travel rewards card until she's paid down her debt. In the future, she plans to use it for large purchases to maximize her miles, ensuring she pays the entire balance each month.

Long-Term:

Sarah will research whether there's a better travel card with higher rewards or lower interest rates that better aligns with her spending habits.

Step 4: Monitor and Adjust

1. **Monthly Review**

   Sarah plans to review her credit card balances, payments, and credit score each month. She'll track her progress toward paying down her balances and increasing her credit score.

2. **Quarterly Review**

   After 3 months, Sarah will reassess her spending and rewards strategy. If her travel rewards card isn't providing enough benefits, she will consider applying for a different card that offers higher rewards or lower fees.

Step 5: Stay Committed to the Game

Sarah commits to sticking with her debt reduction plan while carefully managing her rewards strategy. She understands that discipline is key and will continue to stay informed about credit card offers and rewards programs that may benefit her in the future.

Sarah's Summary:

Current Credit Score: 690

Total Credit Card Debt: $6,500

Goals:

- o **Short-Term**: Pay off $2,000 in 6 months and raise credit score to 720.
- o **Long-Term**: Earn 100,000 travel miles, build credit score to 750+, and avoid carrying balances.

Strategy:

- o Focus on paying off the cashback card debt.
- o Reduce spending on the travel rewards card until debt is paid off.
- o Avoid using the retail store card.
- o Eventually, maximize rewards by using the travel card for big purchases and paying it off each month.

Example 2
Step 1: Assess Your Current Credit Card Situation

Michael's Current Situation

Michael currently has two credit cards:

Card 1:

> **Type:** Cashback Card
> **Credit Limit:** $4,000
> **Current Balance:** $0
> **Interest Rate:** 15% APR
> **Rewards:** 1.5% cash back on all purchases

Card 2:

> **Type:** Travel Rewards Card
> **Credit Limit:** $8,000
> **Current Balance:** $3,000
> **Interest Rate:** 20% APR
> **Rewards:** 3x points on travel, 1x points on everything else

Michael has been managing his credit well, paying more than the minimum payments on his travel card and paying off his cashback card every month. He wants to apply for a new credit card that offers a substantial sign-on bonus and use that bonus to start a brokerage account to invest in the stock market.

Step 2: Define Your Financial Goals

Michael's Financial Goals
1. **Short-Term Goal (next 3 months)**
    a. Apply for a new credit card that offers a sign-on bonus of $500 or more.
    b. Use the bonus to start a brokerage account and make his first investment in stocks.
2. **Long-Term Goal (next 1-3 years)**
    a. Grow his brokerage account to $10,000 through disciplined investing.
    b. Pay off the balance on his travel card in 12 months or less and stop carrying credit card debt entirely.

Step 3: Create Your Credit Card Strategy

Now that Michael has defined his financial goals, he needs to develop a strategy for applying for the right credit card and using it effectively.

1. **Evaluate Current Cards**

    Card 1 (Cashback Card)
    Michael uses this card regularly and pays the balance in full each month. This card is not a priority for change.

    Card 2 (Travel Rewards Card)
    Michael has a $3,000 balance and a 20% APR on this card. He plans to continue making extra payments, but he's also

considering reducing his usage of this card to focus on his new credit card plan.

2. Choosing the Right Credit Card

Michael's primary objective is to find a credit card that offers a large sign-on bonus that he can turn into an investment. Here's his plan:

Sign-On Bonus Requirement:

Look for cards offering at least $500 in cashback or rewards points that can be converted to cash within the first 3 months after meeting a minimum spend.

Considerations

Michael prefers a card with low fees (or a waived annual fee in the first year).

He wants the minimum spend to be reasonable (ideally $3,000-$4,000 in 3 months) so he can achieve it with his regular expenses.

After some research, Michael finds a card offering **$750 in cashback after spending $4,000 in the first 3 months**. It has no annual fee for the first year and offers 1.5% cash back on all purchases. This card will allow him to invest $750 into his brokerage account.

3. **Plan for Spending and Meeting the Bonus**

Michael plans to allocate his regular expenses to meet the $4,000 minimum spend:

Rent: $1,200 per month
Groceries: $500 per month
Utilities and Bills: $300 per month
Other Purchases: $200 per month

With these regular expenses, he can quickly meet the spending requirement in 2.5 months, without making unnecessary purchases.

4. **Maximize the Sign-On Bonus**:

Once Michael receives the $750 cashback, he will transfer it to his bank account and fund his new brokerage account. He plans to start investing in a diversified portfolio of stocks and exchange-traded funds (ETFs) with the goal of long-term growth.

Step 4: Monitor and Adjust

1. **Monthly Review**
   Michael will review his credit card balances and payments each month to ensure he's on track to pay off his travel rewards card and manage his new credit card.
2. **Quarterly Review**

He'll also track his progress in the stock market, assessing how his initial investment is performing. Additionally, he will decide whether to keep his new credit card after the first year, if it comes with an annual fee, or if the rewards are still valuable for him.

Step 5: Stay Committed to the Game

Michael commits to using his credit cards strategically to reach his financial goals. He'll be disciplined in paying off his credit card balances each month to avoid interest charges. His goal is to avoid using credit cards for unnecessary spending, focusing instead on how they can be tools for earning bonuses and rewards that help him build wealth.

Michael's Summary:

Current Credit Score: 720

Total Credit Card Debt: $3,000

Goals:

- o **Short-Term:** Apply for a new card, earn $750 in cashback, and use it to invest in the stock market.
- o **Long-Term:** Build his brokerage account to $10,000 and pay off his credit card debt in full within 12 months.

Strategy:

- o Apply for a credit card with a high sign-on bonus.
- o Meet the minimum spend with regular expenses.
- o Use the bonus for an investment account.
- o Pay off travel card debt while maximizing rewards.

Example 3
Step 1: Assess Your Current Credit Card Situation

Emily's Current Situation

Emily is an entrepreneur planning to launch her online boutique. She needs initial capital for inventory, marketing, and website development. Instead of seeking a traditional business loan, she wants to leverage her personal credit by applying for a 0% APR credit card for 15 months to fund her startup expenses.

Currently, Emily has two credit cards:

Card 1:

Type: Cashback Card
Credit Limit: $6,000
Current Balance: $500
Interest Rate: 14% APR
Rewards: 2% cash back on dining and 1% on all other purchases

Card 2:

Type: Travel Rewards Card
Credit Limit: $10,000
Current Balance: $2,000
Interest Rate: 18% APR
Rewards: 3x points on travel and 1x points on everything else

Emily's Evaluation:

She manages her current credit well, consistently making more than the minimum payment. Her credit utilization ratio is low (20%), and her credit score is 740. She wants to avoid taking on high-interest debt to fund her business and sees the 0% APR card as a strategic move.

Step 2: Define Your Financial Goals

Emily's Financial Goals:
1. **Short-Term Goal (next 3 months):**
   a. Apply for a 0% APR credit card with at least 15 months of no interest on purchases.
   b. Use the credit line to fund her online boutique, covering inventory and marketing expenses up to $5,000.
2. **Long-Term Goal (next 15 months):**
   a. Generate enough revenue from her business to pay off the credit card balance in full before the promotional 0% APR period ends.
   b. Grow her boutique's monthly income to at least $4,000 by the end of the 15-month period.

Step 3: Create Your Credit Card Strategy

Now that Emily has clear financial goals, she can create a strategy for using her new 0% APR credit card effectively.

1. **Evaluate Current Cards**

    Card 1 (Cashback Card):
    Emily uses this card for everyday expenses and consistently pays it off in full. It has a low balance, so she plans to keep using it for personal expenses.

    Card 2 (Travel Rewards Card):
    With a balance of $2,000, Emily is working to pay this down. She doesn't have to rush since her focus will be on leveraging the new 0% APR card for her business.

2. **Choosing the Right Credit Card**

    Emily needs a card with a long 0% APR introductory period and a credit limit that is high enough to cover her business needs. Here's her plan:

    0% APR Requirement:
    Find a card that offers 0% APR for at least 15 months on purchases. This will allow her to make her business purchases without incurring interest.

Credit Limit Consideration:

She needs a credit limit of at least $5,000 to cover her startup costs. Cards with higher limits are preferable, but she will work within her approved limit.

After researching, Emily finds a card that offers **0% APR for 18 months** on purchases with a credit limit of up to $7,500, depending on approval. There's no annual fee, and it offers 1.5% cashback on all purchases, which can help her earn some rewards as she spends.

3. **Plan for Spending and Using the 0% APR Period**

Emily calculates that her startup expenses will be around $5,000, broken down as follows:

Inventory: $2,500
Website Development: $1,200
Marketing and Advertising: $800
Miscellaneous Costs (Shipping, Packaging, etc.): $500

She will use the new 0% APR card for all business expenses and set up a detailed budget to ensure she stays within her credit limit.

4. **Payoff Strategy**

Since Emily has 18 months of no interest, she wants to ensure her business generates enough revenue to pay off the balance before the 0% APR period ends. She plans to pay down the card in monthly installments once the business starts generating income:

Target Payoff Time:

15 months (even though the 0% APR lasts for 18 months, she wants a buffer).

Required Monthly Payment:

To pay off $5,000 in 15 months, she will need to make **$334 monthly payments**. She estimates her business will start generating enough revenue by month 3 to cover this amount.

Step 4: Monitor and Adjust

1. **Monthly Review**

   Emily will track her business expenses and income each month. If the business generates more revenue than expected, she will increase her monthly payments to pay the balance sooner.

2. **Quarterly Review**

   Every 3 months, she will review her business performance. If the boutique isn't generating enough revenue by month 3, she will explore other financing options (such as a small business loan) to avoid carrying a balance past the 0% APR period.

Step 5: Stay Committed to the Game

Emily is committed to using her 0% APR card responsibly to fund her business. She understands the importance of paying off the balance before the 0% APR period ends to avoid interest charges, which would quickly erode her profits. She also plans to remain disciplined in her spending, only using the card for business-related expenses.

Emily's Summary:

    Current Credit Score: 740

    Total Credit Card Debt: $2,500 (including balances on existing cards)

    Goals:

-     **Short-Term**: Apply for a 0% APR card to cover $5,000 in startup costs for her business.
-     **Long-Term**: Pay off the credit card balance within 15 months and grow her boutique to generate $4,000 monthly income.

    Strategy:

-     Use the 0% APR card exclusively for business expenses.
-     Pay off the balance before the promotional period ends by budgeting $334 in monthly payments from business revenue.

The following chart shows the sample credit card breakdowns for Sarah, Michael, and Emily. Study the side-by-side comparisons and find the best plan that works for your financial situation.

Assessment Step	Sarah's Plan	Michael's Plan	Emily's Plan
Step 1: Assess Current Credit Card Situation	- **Cards:** 3 (Cashback, Travel Rewards, Retail Store) - **Debt:** $6,500 - **Score:** 690 - Managing high balances on Travel card	- **Cards:** 2 (Cashback, Travel Rewards) - **Debt:** $3,000 - **Score:** 720 - Focused on reducing Travel card debt	- **Cards:** 2 (Cashback, Travel Rewards) - **Debt:** $2,500 - **Score:** 740 - Avoiding high-interest debt for business startup
Step 2: Define Financial Goals	- **Short-Term:** Pay off $2,000 in 6 months, raise score to 720 - **Long-Term:** Earn 100,000 miles, score 750+	- **Short-Term:** Earn $750 cashback for investment - **Long-Term:** Grow brokerage to $10,000, pay off debt	- **Short-Term:** Get 0% APR card for $5,000 startup - **Long-Term:** Pay off in 15 months, grow revenue to $4,000/month
Step 3: Create Credit Card Strategy	- Prioritize paying off Cashback card - Limit use of Travel card - Avoid Retail card	- Apply for new card with bonus - Use rewards for investment - Reduce spending on Travel card	- Use 0% APR card for business expenses - Create repayment plan - Use existing cards for personal expenses
Step 4: Monitor and Adjust	- **Monthly:** Review balances and score - **Quarterly:** Adjust rewards strategy as needed	- **Monthly:** Track debt reduction and investments - **Quarterly:** Reassess card benefits	- **Monthly:** Monitor business expenses and revenue - **Quarterly:** Review credit usage and business growth

Step 5: Stay Committed to the Game	- Focus on reducing debt and maximizing rewards - Stay updated on new offers	- Disciplined use of cards for wealth-building - Avoid unnecessary spending	- Dedicate to paying off debt before 0% APR ends - Prioritize business growth through strategic credit use

The examples of Sarah, Michael, and Emily illustrate how personalized strategies and a thoughtful approach to credit cards can lead to meaningful financial progress. By assessing their unique situations, defining clear goals, and creating tailored strategies, they each found ways to use credit as a tool for growth rather than a burden. Whether tackling debt, maximizing rewards, or using credit to fund a business venture, these scenarios highlight the importance of proactive management, continuous monitoring, and commitment to long-term financial goals. As you consider your own credit journey, let these examples serve as inspiration and practical guides to mastering the credit card game on your terms.

Credit cards are a financial tool, and if you use them wisely, you will win. Therefore, it is crucial to understand the strategies for not just getting the right credit card but knowing the right tools and principles to win the credit card game.